The Rise and Fall of the Cardiff City Valley Rams

By Gwyn Davies

Publisher Annis Abraham Jnr

www.annisabraham.co.uk

Book Cover designed by Owain Davies and Damian Evans

ISBN 978-0-9561339-1-5

First published by Annis Abraham Jnr, 2nd June 2009

Contents

Dedications

*I would like to dedicate this book
to my wife Alison and my three children,
James, Beckie and Ben.*

*And a special mention for my sorely missed best mate
Beefy Jenkins. Four foot eight inches tall,
but a giant of a man.
Whilst I know you are no longer with us,
I also know you have been there for every moment.*

*All monies raised from this book will be used to maintain
the Valley Rams web site and Valley Rams TV.
We will also continue donating to the charities
we support as always.*

Acknowledgments

A big thank you to my wife Alison, for her constant help with proof reading, spell checking and encouragement, tea, coffee and toast.

Annis and Joanne for the encouragement and enthusiasm in getting me here, (enthusiasm another way of saying constant nagging, lol) Topman, big thanks.

Dr. Cliff Stott, for everything and making us feel we weren't on our own.

To Sam Hammam, he made us believe, and a friend forever.

To Steve Borley for being there.

To our FIO Simon Insole, a genuine bloke who must be as frustrated as us.

To Vince Alm the most committed and hardest working Cardiff fan in history.

To Corky a real mate and a great landlord.

To all the bus companies and drivers who more than played their part.

To everyone who sent pictures – Dai Camera, Gezza, Duke, Paul Hillman and Gazzi.

To all the staff at Cardiff City F.C. for their help and support, especially Nashy, Dennis, Kersy, Julian, Suzanne and Mona.

To all the original Rams gang: Jinx, Davis, Big Sam, Mogs, Ketty, Russel Meeke, The Swansons Jumbo, Martyn, Dai Starling, Beefy James, Dean Willis, EVB, Insane Wayne, Keith Peacock. Stickey, Corky, Jack Lewis and Bryan, Payney and Alfie, Roger, Keith and Joe, Dai Taxi, Quinney, Big Steve, Frankie Mason and Dicey, Chris Catterson, BobSpadz, Merv Pearce, Dean Bryncethin (R.I.P.), Gareth, Chief Port Talbot, Macca, Mart the Dart, Ace, Dean Penrhys, Jinx Treherbert, Tony Murray.

To the lads I remember from each area. Apologies to those I have missed out.

Aberdare: Russell & Flicker Meeke, Jeff Hill, Parry, Huw & Shane Bond, Dai Lew and Adam, Jinx, Chris & Nathan. The Starling gang, Gavin, Beefy James, Bernie Arms, Grommett, Forey, Brian, Dennis, Barney, John Jones, Shane and Steven Leeke, Carl Reed, John Collins. Mickey Haven & Crowley, Tiny, Mad Andie, Lakey, Marksy, Shit for brains Cartwright, Needsy, Boring Bob, Clive Bryant, Dan Beynon, Dwttie, Fudge, Gatesy, Ganger, Gareth Ireland, Gary Stckler, Gunger, Jarrad Parry, Jeff Cleaton, Jeff Francis, Kelvin Hancock, Klaus, Tubby Lee, Les Howells, Mal Hinton, Mat Wyatt, Paul Stevens, Peter Jeffries, Rob Jones, Ross Thomas, Steve Pontin, Stuart McGill, Toffa, ony Garthwaite, Tony Panniers, Travolta, Vic James, Dodgey, Mickey Doran.

Mountain Ash & Abercynon: Keith Jumbo Edwards, Perthcelyn Mafia, Dickie, Pugsy, Jimmy Brace, Bramwell, Tony Brown, Doc, Turner, Mike the Bookie and Phil (RIP) and Jacko from the Rhondda. Mount Pleasant Jumbo, Turners the chef, Tuckers, Starchy (RIP), Nigel Weekes, Roger Meadon, Chris Hill, Martin Sanders, Russell (Eddie) Meeke, Mark Carey, Richard and Chris Edwards, Jay, Ben, Alfie, Young Tucks, Kidner, Stokesy, Brian & Peter, Ken Osborn, Paul & Simon Hughes, Mike Clarke, Abercynon Whingers and Moaners Tigger, Brush, Mike Williams, Muffy, Mart the Dart, Phillip Brown, Brian Bonkers, Keith Peacock, Smiler.

Pontypridd: Merv Pearce, Snowy, Coxey, Leckers, Scrumpo, Wardy, Kevin Lew, Phil Sav, Craig Roberts, Huw Withey, Gary Lewis, Dion, Barry Murphy, Gareth and Esther.

Ferndale (formerly known as the Ferndale Freedom Fighters): Mike Stickey Williams, Catty, Crazy, Bubs, Posh, Eddie, Bins, Davies, James, Shaun, Snibs, Dean, Vampy, Big Al, Moulds, Villain, Keks, Elfed, Weazel, Apples, Gazzi, Dap, Gauvers, Pan, Jickey, Bomber, Chudseye, Grant, Tubby, Spike, Mad Jeff, Ribbsy.

Treherbert: Jinx, Robbie Bounds, Cowboy, Apples.

Pandy and Porth: Mog's & Ketty's flock,Terry Lew, Duane, Mario, Gaffa, Seadog, Jay, Dean Penrhys, Brownie, Ronnie Rock, Shawnny, Falmer, Dean(tomato head) Flarty, Evans, Sicey & Sicey junior, Dai Ton, Slicey.

Lower Merthyr: Big Sam's crew, Bonkers, Ted, Richie & Richie Junior, Llantwit Dilwyn, Joey Mullins, Macca, Big Tom, Micky skin, Necky, Mikey Taylor, Oscar, Dai Morales, Hooker (RIP), Keith Andrews, Tuffy, Graham Williams, Dai Troedyrhiw, Stud, Gary Price (RIP), Jason Law, Dai Ginge.

Bryncethin: Gareth, Dean (RIP), Gaffa, Andrew, Paki, Sam, Poples, Gerald The Scorpion, Bunky, Twink, The Toffee Apple Gang – (Etta, Smurf, David & Donut), Neil (Taffs Well), Dil, Adz brothers, Mob, Brendan, Dai Roberts, Squeezy & Joe, Milton, Browny, Teal, Dom, Dai & Eddie, Howard, Bunhead,

Hodge, Dai & Dale, Seal, Bizzy, Stan, Craig, Fly, Lumper, Tom, Lanky, Ian, John, Gerwyn, Lee, Tony, Twisty, Dai Morris, Quiet John, Dicky, Rod, Geoff, Gary Williams, Mark, Johnathan, Rhydian, Lloydy, Pears, Aaron, Blue Mist, Bones, Busy, Dibs, Jock, Morgan, Lewy, Aaron, Fly, Flange
And the Girls – Donna, Joce, Denise, Mrs Paki, Kim, Caroline, Barbara, Sue.

Port Talbot: Chief's crowd, Jamesy boy Sharney, Picky, Deano, Bully, Jaffa, Lamby, Jenners, Big bird, Skunk, Mammys boy, Bowman, Rob.

Doe a Deer crew: Martyn Payne, Alfie Annan, Smedger, Alf Garnet, Jacko Martin, Brian, Yorkie, Snappers, Sadam, Richie, Jamie, Disco Des, C, Terry Harris, Evo, Martin and John (The Coppers), Dai Gas, Shane Pearce, Lloyd and Dean Griffiths, T-Bone, M Gardiner (Bear), Mike Hagan, Mike Gale, Garry Way, Frank Humphreys, Richard Humphreys, Paul Gammon, Steve Elliot, Eric Harmer, Terry, Whitcombe, David Whitcombe (Biffo), Tony Moriarty (Mo), Graham Oliver, Ollie, Nathan and Kevin, Andrew Phillips, Dean Hurley, Craig Phillps, Steve Watkin, Antony Chessari (from Lyon), Alex George, John Gulley.

Big mention for Liz the only female who still travels today and Martyns Auntie who has more pubs in the UK than Brains.

Barry: Quinneys crew, Donald, Des, Dickie, Captain Gutsful, Dicky Doughnut, Stary, Karl Tillman, Spud, Joey, Podgey.

Canton and Central Cardiff: Keith Harmans crew, Jo and little Jo, The Badger, Matthew, and Andrew, Tony, Gareth and Phil Storer, Techno Terry, and Digital Dave, Russ, Andy, Richard, Simmo, Michael and Jimmy The Youth, The General, Val, Mark and Carl, Chuggy, and Semi, Dolphy (RIP). Wilson and the Llanrumney boys. Ruddy, Owain, Phil, Biscuit, Spikey, Dionne, German Shepherd and finally our driver Tudor.

Cardiff East: Dai Taxi's crew, Harry Potter, Swampy No Arse, Dai Burger, Waller, Luke, Cael, Evan, Midge, Midgeano, arvo, Wez, Dylan, Russ, Andy, Ritchie, Spud, Ruddy, Morgans, Hugh, Scroat, Pongo, Bomber, Bob G.

Grand Slam: Big Steve Rowlands and his bro Paul, Woody, Dave the Rave, Andrew, Steety Les Millward, Terry, Scurrey, Sweety, Tall Mark, Jammo, Stress, Big G, Hazy, Reggie, Gnosher, Jason, Luke, Alistair, Rab, Wally, Streety, Leroy, Tallis, Bomber, Lemon.

Cwmbran & Newport: Frank Mason, Tony Murray, Spike, Leachy, Howler, Freeman, Magic, Tewy, Geordie, Youngy, Rawlings, Richie, Arnie, Tony Spelloni, Yom, Andy from Maindee, Risca boys big Dai and Hoppy. Rawlings. Magor Massive: Andy Pit Bull, Phyllis, Clarkey, Derrick Williams.

Merthyr & Heads of the Valley: Jack Lewis and Bryan's bus, Carlton Beynon, the Foley boys, Andrew, Chris & Rob, Sticksy, One punch, Paul, John & Darren Thomas, Brecon Mossy (RIP), Dilly Whan (RIP), Steve, Shakey, Shaun, Nicky Morgan, Alyn, Chris & Tony Flynn, Alistair & Rob Hamilton.

Rhymney: Titch, Hoppy, Ginner, Wynn, Alec, Percy.

Tredegar: Spazy, Garkey, Downsey, Mark, Big Ken, Cocco & his son (RIP), Slcey, George, Bubbles.

Ebbw Vale: Clive, Essex, Gomez, Wayne Bevan, Bolton, Gully, Drunken Drummer.

Cwm: Nigel & Andrew Williams.

Brynmawr: Dean & Zayner.

Abergavenny: John, Hugh, Rhys, Andrew & Rob.

Llandovery: Alec & Andrew.

Forest of Dean: Paul & Mike.

Northampton: Andy Williams & his crew.

Nelson: Captain Corkys ship mates, Peter & Geraint, Jumbo, Glen, Gareth & Gerwyn Edwards, Kerry Jones, Mel Pearce, Big Dean Beecham, Chris & Rhys Bullock, Richard Cox (Coxy), Mark Engwell (Engy), Steve Hindley, Mike Denham, Scott Jones, Adam Price, Ashley Jones, Daniel McCarthy, Barry Philips (Baz), Shaun Windows, Keith James (Penfold), Gareth John, Barry Lewton, Gary Jones (Popeye), Peter Szpadt, Jeremy Wilson, Kerry Pickett, Matthew Astley.

Bargoed: Melanie Rich the only girl who could control the "Battle Bus" Daintons; Gareth (who is ALWAYS right?) and Huw (aka porn star moustache), Sue Dainton. The Cheeky girls Nia and Bethan Jordan, Luke, Mark Dainton and his mate Dr Childish. lenor, Mia and Evan. Dainton senior (Winston). Darryl – Captain Pugwash, Brian, Mark, Hodges, Burchy Plus Morgan. The Alan Bodman brigade: Geraint Bodman, Alun Bodman, Chris Bodman, Garth (miserable one), Mike Beasley (aka Les Dawson), Andy Rees, Selwyn Williams, Babes Crap Shag (Craig), Tich, Ben, Selwyn, Matthew and Byron Farr, Maynard, Uncle Albert, Tony Jones (aka The German), Vaughan Jones Shadowy Figure of Chaos The Tuckers, Daniel and Jake Veale, Dai Faulkner, Grant Lewis, Dai Gibbins, Lee Coles, Sanders, Daniel Cook, Luke and Ross Snellgrove, Brian's kids, Matthew Astley and Kelvin Pickett – Magnus

Magnesun, Adam and Andy Craig (the Sailor), Astley and Hannah, Matthew (Muffers), Whiskey.

AHM: Chris 'tex' Catterson, Dai Dullandy, Isaacs, tumpo, aggro, chopper aka horrible ives, Mike 'the general' Ford Tucker, Dai Camera, Guto King, Shotty, Clarkey, Ozzy, Dean Hurley, Dom Towell, Nobby Harding, Browny, Jordan Gurner, Muffy, Nelly Phillips, Ginger, Johnny Adler, loopy Lewis, Compo, Shaz, Brideux, Gethyn, Skym, Red Crane, John Harries, Bubble, Chunks, Spike, Frosty, Dai Thompson, Harry Potter, Matt Thornton, Lee Jon, Sid Whatley, Daddows, Dennis James, Isty, Mike Heath, Cheesey, Gary Morgan, Dai Thomas & The Banshees, the old grey tossers, Steptoe the driver.

Chunkys boys Rhydfelin: Chunky, Chris Godwin, Condo, Liam, Trot, Mario, Ozzy, Dai, Blacker, Greg Weygood, Spike, Damian, Wilshire, Penel, Nicky Jones, Richy, Broadway, Dai Grif, Mark Owens, Clive Jones, Sid Sullivan, Paul Elly, Dean Evans.

The Ely Valley Sunshine bus: Mike the landlord of the Squirrel, Insane Wayne, Gezza, Simon EVB, Shaun the Anti-Christ, Kenny Ham, Deacon, Reecey, Gee, Keith Greenslade, Dai Ambler, Mayo, Rooney, Dai Gould, Egg, Donkey, Stupid, The Beasley Boys Stu & Steve, Cooky, Hutchy, Tunner, Rob the Drive, Dai Adams, SBF1, Jamie Sian & Lloyd Webb, The Dando's Mike, Rob & Kev, Minto, Ozzy the Bluebird, Poth, Murphy, Will, Huw, Owen, Nev, Dewi, Adam, Scott, Sarah, Shakey, Quinney.

The Landsdowne Gang: Roger Jenkins, Lloydey (Rowlands), Nigel Blues, Alan Parsons, John Davies, Kevin Geach, Macker (Pete) & Son, Norm, Scouse, Eddie The Pub Singer, Mark, Lee Ledley (Jones' brother), Jock, Sandra & Hilary, Zoe Jones & dad, Dio Nicholas, Peter The Lansdowne D.J., Indian Darren, his home-made food ... & special cakes! Hickie & Bethan, Darren & Amanda, Lee Hutchings, Dean Hurley & his crew. Whitchurch Kev and his mates, The 2 Jo's, Gareth & Donna, The Harris Seniors.

Introduction

I HAD BEEN asked by quite a few people on quite a few occasions to put together a book covering the period of the Rams existence. Luckily or unluckily depending on which way you view the book, out of all those asking me, Annis Abrahams junior was the most persistent. His help, enthusiasm and encouragement throughout this exercise have been priceless. And the experience he has gained with his already published mini library has been a great help.

The Rams came about at the right time for me. I'd always been heavily involved in taking part in sport. I had played basketball at quite a high level. I had been a member of the British Judo team and have travelled all around the world representing the country for some twelve years and then at the age of 30 when the judo demands became too much, I took to playing rugby for what was meant to be a past time and outlet for someone with my energy. I progressed through the ranks and for a couple of years played at quite a high level culminating with two seasons at Pontypridd RFC. I finally retired from rugby at age 38, when I realised it was taking me longer to put on my strappings and dressings than it was to actually play a game. I had never stopped watching Cardiff City through all these periods of activity and now I had the opportunity to devote even more time to my first love which was football (this is possibly why I've had so many ex wives along the way).

The next five years or so were taken up with driving mini buses, transit vans etc, booking occasional coaches and just having fun watching city week in week out. But then along came Sam Hamman and the need for some of us to step up to the mark were established. The rest is history and hopefully this book will catalogue some of those events. It is sad that the Rams no longer organise away travel, we still run an internet site, Valley Rams T.V. and a message board. And all those involved still feel part of the biggest, closest and best bunch of friends you could ever hope to meet. What we created still runs but on a fragmented format and a lot of people who ran coaches for us during this period, are still running them to this day. The politics, frustration and unlevel playing field was one of the main reasons we cease to organise travel. My worry is that in future years away travel will be organised by a select few for a select few and if you have so much as a speeding fine or parking ticket on your record you will be excluded from this group. The sort of people that were travelling with us may not be welcome in this new group and in all honesty, if I was at a function with my grandparents and close family I wouldn't want to be sitting next to half of them. But saying that they aren't bad people, they are the salt of the earth and changing the make-up of the type of fans who watch Cardiff city week in, week out thereby excluding some of the above, would be the end of football as far as I'm concerned.

Gwyn Davies, 1st June, 2009

Foreword

Reading the riot act!

I started writing this foreword with a sense of what has a bloke like me – an academic in his mid forties - got to offer a book like this? After all, this book is about fans of Cardiff City Football Club, perhaps one of the most renowned set of fans in the country, if not the world. At first glance this book could easily appear to be another in a long line of publications of a genre I call 'hooliporn'. But when you get into this book you will begin to realise it is so much more than that. For me, it's actually a detailed record of one of the most important fan movements in recent years – the Valley RAMs. It's a book that documents the struggles of a group of Cardiff fans and their attempt to face up to the reality of what the so called 'hooligan problem' at Cardiff is actually all about. A powerful story not least of all because it's told from the perspective of those involved. So perhaps its not so strange that I was asked to write this foreword and for me it was certainly an honour not least of all because I hold Gwyn in such high regard.

But at first I couldn't work out what to say, but as I was thinking this through Carrick scored for United, the Sky TV cameras shot across to their now ecstatic fans. Given that victory at Wigan meant they were now just one point away from the Premiership the fans were in total, unrestrained and triumphant joy. Most of those that I could see were 'lads', and to be there would have meant that most if not all were regular travellers with United. There were fists in the air, shaking them at the camera, with grimaces all aimed I'm sure at any on-looking Liverpool fans. But despite these outward signs of aggression the overriding emotion was expressed by grown men hugging and the universal smiles – it was simple, mass pleasure in total bedlam. All were already standing when the goal went in and in this moment of ultimate joy those at the back were diving over the seats, some in the crowd were falling forward. But the moment was soon over and I'm sure nobody was hurt in the melee. It was this that captured what in many ways this 'hooligan' stuff is all about, 'lads' pushing the boundaries in the pursuit of those little zones of collective pleasure.

Above and beyond that fact the United fans were doing what a large chunk of football fans go to football to experience - the unbridled and unrestrained joy of going ape shit en masse when an important goal goes in. In those moments no one cares about whether standing disrupts a 'sight line', no one cares if jumping up and down is 'dangerous', nobody cares whether diving over bodies in front of

The Rise and Fall of the Cardiff City Valley Rams

you is going to 'hurt' anyone. Nobody cares if they get knocked over when another fan is going mental with joy because your team's just taken an important result in the eighty sixth minute. Nobody apart from the authorities of course; because at those very moments the eagle eyes of the establishment start to hone in on 'the disruption'. Those that are standing are seen as posing a danger of 'self harm' and disrupting the 'customer care' of some hypothetical pensioner who may want to be sitting in the middle of this autonomous zone of football madness rather than tucked safely away to the sides. In these moments of chaos 'the lads' are seen as 'causing disorder'. Now don't get me wrong. I never have and never would deny that within football crowds there can be some pretty unpleasant individuals. Nor do I think that it is not important to make football a place where anyone can go without fear of threat, intimidation of harm. I welcome the ever growing and diverse mix of people that have moved us away from the surgical masked Millwall fans and terrace taking in the dark days of the seventies.

The differences are not about what we want but how we get there. And in this sense this book is in many ways a 'first'. It's a combination of funny stories about the laughs to be had being a Cardiff fan. It's about the characters. The mad almost surreal moments that even the best of comedy writers in the land could never dream of in thousand years. For me this reflects that it is humour rather than conflict that is the defining characteristic of the dedicated fan. I have heard and see some of the sharpest, most intelligent and best timed humour in football crowds and a few of these comedy moments are contained in the following pages.

But we all know football can be a violent place. So this too is also a book about the scrapes, the battles and the narrow escapes witnessed first-hand. But at the same time it's not just another 'bullshit book'. It's not a book that seeks to glorify this violence. Its not about a 'firm' that tries to stand up and pretend to be the most original or the hardest group of 'lads' in the Leagues of England and Wales. It's not a book that should be called 'we came, we saw we conquered'. It's actually a book that also has a serious message about how the vast majority of fans who simply love football end up in situations where violent confrontation seems as though it can't be avoided even though these fans never actively sought conflict out in the first place. It is a story about the solidarity of the Valley's and how this can flow into situations of conflict when others seek to 'bring it on'. It is also a story about how some within the Cardiff contingent actively seek out confrontations in the pursuit of pleasure and reputation. But more importantly than all this it's a true story about how all these things fit together and the authorities can fail to develop a solution to the violence even when a solution to their problems is handed to them on a plate by fans themselves.

Much of that history is contained in the following pages so I won't cover it here. But it all began when Gwynn, and the other characters you will come to know, had a vision of a club they love that was in crisis, stuck in the lower divisions in a stadium that was falling apart. They knew that the fans had struggled against the authorities for years and were seen as the enemy rather than the lifeblood of the club. The antagonism was mutual. But then along came one of the biggest mavericks in football, the Ayatollah himself, Sam 'the man'

Hamman. Sam had a vision of a new twenty first century club in a new twenty first century stadium. His arrival coincided with the development of the RAMs but it was to prove a powerful coincidence. Sam was if anything a pragmatic man so he and everybody else knew that a new stadium could only happen if the Cardiff fans did something to drive out the violence from their midst. It was critical that Cardiff F.C. could become a club that was more attractive to a wider fan base across South Wales and as such more appealing as an investment to the money men that would be essential to achieving this goal. But Sam was different. He understood that the solution lay in an alliance with the fans, to make them feel a sense of ownership in the club. He wanted them to realise they were as much a part of the solution as they were a part of the problem.

It was Gwynn and the RAMs that I believe were central to delivering the Promised Land. I first met Gwynn in a car-park on the M1 in late 2004. In tow he had about twenty coaches of RAM's and they were on their way to Elland Road. We all know that a Leeds versus Cardiff fixture so soon after the 'riots' at Ninian Park was always going to pose problems. But there were the Cardiff fans, all working with the club and the police to make the opportunity for Cardiff fans to attend this fixture without having to 'mob up' against the Leeds. As they waited to be escorted by the police to the stadium it was obvious that while there were the 'pop and crisp' brigade there were numbers of lads on the busses that were more inclined to 'coke' than they were to 'cola'. There were many there that would have eagerly grasped an opportunity to 'kick off' if it was delivered to them. But at the same time almost all of the fans there had other priorities and that was simply to have a good day out, getting tanked up, letting off some steam, and doing so without causing any harm to anybody else but themselves. It wasn't that they were hiding from trouble they were just actively working together to avoid it.

What I soon came to understand was that it was no accident that practically the whole Cardiff 'Category B' contingent was on the RAMs busses that day and that it was no small success that Gwynn, the other RAMs organisers, the club and the police, had delivered them to this car-park. As it turned out the RAMs came and went from Elland Road without one of them getting involved in any trouble. For the Leeds fans it was a different story. Only weeks before Leeds fans had rioted outside the stadium when the police stopped them from attacking the entire contingent of Millwall fans. The Cardiff fixture saw another big 'turn –out' and once again unable to get to the Cardiff the Leeds contingent of nutters and scum bags once again rioted outside. For me this was more about the Leeds 'lads' wanting to attack the Old Bill and were simply using these matches as their opportunity. A few months after, a few doors went in and around twenty five of the Leeds rioters were jailed. But throughout the Cardiff fans kept themselves inside Elland Road. Once the police had driven the rioters down Elland Road the RAMs were free to load up the beer onto their busses and piss off back to South Wales after a good day out (apart from losing one nil of course!). The enduring image was Gwyn's minibus flying around the car park of Elland Road dropping off slabs of cans onto each RAMs coach despite the fact that it was illegal for those on the busses to drink; an active blind eye from the West Yorkshire Police as a 'thank you' to the fans of Cardiff City F.C.

I then went on to watch many Cardiff matches over the next few years as the RAMs initially went from strength to strength. The strategy was simple. Offer all the lads the easiest way to get from the Valleys and Cardiff to the match. Put beer on the busses so they can enjoy the journey and find them a pub to go to where they can relax without getting harassed by the local idiots. Get them to the ground, in and out and away back to Wales with some beer to stop them stopping off and being surrounded by the various temptations of being mob handed in an off licence. Not complicated just the kind of thing you need to do to get those that might be tempted by violence tempted by a stronger force of having a good day out with the lads in pursuit of the collective pleasures that the United fans so powerfully displayed at Wigan. And from a police perspective this was really something else. Gone were the days of mass riots involving Cardiff. Gone was the need for cops to find the various groups of roaming Cardiff 'lads' arriving from every which way. Gone was the risk of sporadic disorder all over the town centres. Gone was the need for cops to bring out their batons, well at least for the Cardiff fans. Where else could they get five hundred 'risk' fans delivering themselves compliantly into the stadium without any hint of disorder? And when the police took the bait and worked to deliver the RAMs strategy things went well.

If only life were that simple, because in the background there was a whole series of other issues going on. It was always a struggle to keep a whole mob of 'Category B's' together on these busses and happy at the same time. In fact it was a full time job. But the authorities often didn't make this any easier. Take for example the behaviour of the Football Licensing Authority representative who following the Cardiff fans good behaviour at the Leeds fixture forced a situation in which Cardiff were docked ticket allocation for the following year as a consequence of them standing during the match. But the entire contingent of Leeds fans in the opposite stand stood throughout the same match without any consequences whatsoever and around one hundred and fifty of them went on to riot outside! Where was the logic in that? For many of the RAMs this was simply a kick in the teeth for behaving themselves. Of course, it's currently illegal to drink on coaches going to or from a designated football match. And when things began the cops were in the main happy to let the RAMs drink on the busses because of the benefits it delivered. It seemed an obvious trade off, let them drink and they won't riot. But for some the sight of a mob of Cardiff fans contravening this minor law was like a red rag to a bull. There was the sense that it was a necessity to control them, to corral them, and most of all never to be 'told what to do' by them.

When the RAMs made it clear that it was a simple equation - facilitate them and avoid problems some police forces took this as threat. For them the police were in charge and despite the fact that nobody was disputing this some forces could not help themselves but to make that fact perfectly clear. It would get ridiculous. Wayne Nash, another payer in this story, told me one of the funniest stories about one of Cardiff's first visits to the Britannia Stadium after the major riots in 2000. The cops met them on the coaches and forced them to go to a pub nearby where they left them to drink for an hour or so. Of course the publican was made up and was laughing all the way to the bank. Cardiff fans were happy to do this, of course, that's partly why they were there in the first place. So into the pub they go and start necking back the beers. As the match approached the cops loaded them back onto the busses and then took them around the roundabout before pulling the busses over. A cop gets onto the bus and says 'we have reason to believe you've been drinking'. In true sarcastic fashion the shout comes back in a full on South Wales accent 'Well no shit Sherlock!'. And there it was, how contradictory can you be? You put football fans in pubs and then use the fact that they have been drinking against them. Other forces were worse and I will leave Gwyn to give you the gory detail.

But none the less the RAMs were really delivering a solution through keeping the mass contingent on the busses, not by trickery but by making life easier for them. However you want to look at the situation there was a transformation going on and Cardiff fans were posing less and less of a threat. The endless cycle of disorder was being broken. Those within the Cardiff fan base who did want to create problems were becoming more marginalised and had less of the numbers they needed to take on the other firms. If and when they tried to cause problems Cardiff fans would help to marginalise and 'self police' them. It wasn't a perfect solution, it didn't totally avoid problems but it certainly reduced them. In this way it was streets ahead of anything I have seen or heard of in England and Wales and held out for real opportunities for long term reductions in the levels of hooliganism surrounding Cardiff City F.C..

But as the threat was decreasing so too were the goal posts moving. Cardiff lads who previously could have a good day out were starting to get picked up for minor offences like 'attempting drunk entry'. The FLA was attacking them for standing up. Some police forces would not let them have drink on the busses. Those travelling on the busses started to complain that 'in the old days they would have left us alone'. The authorities were happy enough to keep them contained there was no interest in minor offences. But now the threat was subsiding they could start addressing the drink culture that was so central the RAMs but such an issue for the authorities. The threat they posed carried its own reward. Soon it was becoming more and more difficult to get the lads onto the busses. Why should they travel on the coaches only to be bubbled up, denied a drink and herded around from pillar to post? After all they were perfectly free to travel by train or car and drink as much as they liked without reprimand. True they may well not get in if they couldn't walk but otherwise they knew that drinking heavily wouldn't be a problem. There was no clear and obvious reason for why it was that one force would accommodate the RAMs, allow them to drink, provide a pub – even in one case a whole town centre – to drink in before the match. While for another no drinks would be allowed, no beer would be served in the stadium and the overarching style of policing was confrontational from the outset. This lack of consistency and hospitality then started to undermine the

The Rise and Fall of the Cardiff City Valley Rams

RAMs leadership. They were becoming less and less able to deliver the solution that everybody wanted. Then after years of building it became too much, the leadership gave up and the RAMs collapsed

By now the planning of the new stadium was well advanced. But the money men were never going to invest with Sam at the helm. He fell on his sword and walked out only to end up in legal wrangles with the new owners. Peter Risdale was seen as a safe pair of hands. After all he had overseen the collapse of the once mighty Leeds United so here was a man who really knew how things could go wrong. The money came in. The new Stadium is no longer a dream and Cardiff were only goal difference off a shot at the Premiership this time around. Despite this rosy story on the pitch there is a powerful lesson to be learnt in the pages of this book about what goes on off it. A story about how a movement of fans could put forward a genuine solution to a problem only to be destroyed by the inability of the authorities to build a genuine and consistent response. Things may well be looking up at Cardiff but to me none of this would have been possible without the Valley RAMs. The fact the RAMs are no more says more about a failure of the authorities to build a realistic approach to the problems of football 'disorder' than it does about Cardiff fans themselves. I hope this book helps to tell us all about what a realistic solution might just look like.

Doctor Clifford Stutt
(Senior Lecturer in Psychology, Liverpool University)
Advisor to the Football League and Home Office
and The Police Authority
1st June, 2009

Chapter 1
The early days

"Gwyn! It's Mogs, where the hell are you? It's coming on top of us. Where are the lads?"

Welcome to Tottenham, the big time and a wake up call for a lot of us. This was our biggest trip as the Valley Rams, or rather the Cardiff and Valley Rams, because what we had started less than a year earlier, and what was intended to be a travel club where we booked a coach or two on a regular basis to pick us up from an area covering 3 of the largest valleys, had now turned into a juggernaut resulting in this Milk cup tie at White Hart Lane on a Tuesday night and 32 coach loads of Rams making the trip up the M4.

Before you start picking up on actual dates and times of these events, I'll apologise now, I don't remember or store such details. I can remember loads of stupid irrelevant facts, but details such as dates, even results and scores, just pass me by like fleeting thoughts. If you want a history book then buy one, if you want a made up story book, then I believe the Jack Army still has a few left on the shelf. I don't intend lying or making up stories, but dates and times, who gives a fuck.

I had been the catalyst for setting up the Valley Rams some time in 2000. Years previously, there had been other groups such as Adar Glas, who originally were a break off faction of the Official supporters club and drew on their support mostly from the Valley towns surrounding Cardiff. They had run for many years and the now sadly deceased married couple Roy and Mair Daniels, who looked after this group were real legendary characters. Don't worry about the ICF or the Headhunters, Mair Daniels would have seen them all off with her fold-up brolley.

Unfortunately this group had broken up quite a few years earlier but the memories and tales get better every time you recollect or tell them. But the time to reform was ripe. Sam Hamman had taken charge of the club. What a heady mix, the maddest club owner and what some reckoned were the maddest fans in the football league.

We didn't form up because of Sam, but what he had helped to do was enthuse so many people, not just the fans, but the press and media as well. Cardiff were making headlines everywhere, some waiting for us all to fuck up, some hoping we could advance up the divisions and bring some of the benefits to the area that go along with having a successful team in your area. Let's be honest if places like Ipswich and Norwich had never had successful football teams at certain periods, the only other people that would have heard of them were the Vikings or Romans out for a bit of plunder.

Cardiff was a big City; a Capital City (had to remind the Jacks about that). We had a support catchment area of at least a million and a half people to draw on. We were one of the largest areas without a successful team in the league. Fuck me, Blackburn Rovers are in the Premiership and they have a population of 120,000, the Rhondda Valley on its own has a population of close on 100,000. So, what were we doing stuck at the bottom of the second division (old Fourth division) with crowds of 4,000 and looking like we may go out of the league or worse even go bust, what had gone wrong?

We, the fans had to accept some of the blame. We had a fearsome reputation. What investor or company sponsor would touch us with a barge pole. We had in the past, been shafted and stitched up by so many owners, in it for the wrong reasons (as we found at to our cost at later dates and always after the event). The sort of people who had been in charge, were there to try and make money off us, or to massage their egos and profiles. Lots of them got their fingers burnt, or windows smashed, but that's another story. Some of them did actually manage to drain some milk from the cash cow that was no longer producing milk.

Luckily, immediately prior to Sam Hamman coming in, we had a chairman Steve Borley who was a local lad. He'd grown up as a dyed in the wool fan. He was doing well in his steel construction business, but was struggling to plug the financial leaks that were popping up all over the club. How Steve's wife stuck by him at some of these times I'll never know. He must have re-mortgaged his house more times than a Park Lane hotel on a Monopoly board.

I'm sure she couldn't have known half of what was going on or the sacrifices he was making to save his beloved club, or what some women would describe as his little hobby. We will never be able to thank that family enough for keeping us going during some of our worse times.

Jumping forward a bit, I remember after we had beaten QPR in the play off final at the Millennium stadium, the players and the board came out on to the pitch, and Sam being the showman was milking it all, and fair do's to him for getting us that far, but in the background walking quietly behind but with a smile like a Cheshire cat and glowing with pride was Borley. He was no longer centre stage or the main attraction, but he must have felt so proud knowing what he had done, and the part he had played to get his and our club to this stage. Steve is still there and working flat out behind the scene and letting other people take the credit, often for work that he's put in, but that's Steve and whilst he's still involved, a lot of us feel a lot happier and safer knowing that he has ours and the clubs best interest at heart. Mind you, when he retires and takes a well earned rest, he must write a book, that would be a guaranteed must read for all Cardiff fans, some of the goings on that he's seen would blow our socks off, I'm sure.

If we, the fans were partly to blame for some of the clubs problems, what and how could we change things and help the club we claimed to love, yet we had let them down so many times in the past.

I can't point fingers and blame anyone. I had been there and been part of it through all the mad years, and yes whilst I would never describe myself as a "Hoolie" I was very much aware of how things were.

Without deliberately intending to, I had been caught up in situations on many occasions, often after watching another shocking performance. The last thing we needed was to be confronted by a baying mob of rival fans giving us even more grief. Sometimes, it was a real relief to be able to let off a bit of steam and pent up anger on such a mob. Whilst I have witnessed and been part of such events on many occasions, one thing I have never taken part in was the mindless destruction of property. Whilst I could try and justify having a tear up with some rival fans and others will say there is never a justification for such actions, well each to their own and I'm a big believer in Karma and what goes around comes around. I have never bullied any rival fans, and would do anything I could to prevent it happening, but sometimes if someone was looking for it, they didn't have to look too far when Cardiff were around. On the other hand as is now much more the case, treat us properly and with respect, and in most cases we will reciprocate.

But I could never understand or start to justify wanton damage and destruction of property, no matter how badly we had played, or even how badly the ref had robbed us. Smashing windows tipping over cars and wrecking pubs etc. was not the answer.

All this did was give more ammunition to the press and police that we were little better than animals, or as that frothing at the mouth Leeds fan said after their well documented cup defeat "they were like savages from a third world country."

We were caught up in a vicious circle; the worse we behaved the worse we were treated. The more police were called for, the more our reputation deteriorated (or improved, depending on your agenda) the more trouble we would encounter from rival clubs looking for a scalp or another step up on the hooligan league table. And if truth be told, a lot of us more than likely thought at times, "well the team are never going to top any table, but at least our hooligans can", and whilst I can't believe I'm writing this down, if lots of us are honest, it really is how it was, and many amongst us felt any recognition was better than being ignored. I remember seeing a dog trainer saying that a dog would rather be shouted at or slapped than ignored. At least if they couldn't get any loving attention, they were getting some attention, and letting their owners know they were there. Nothing to them could be worse than not feeling acknowledged or part of things. Well at Cardiff we were well and truly part of things.

Even Steve Borley who we saw as one of us, was helpless to stop this vicious circle getting bigger and bigger and rolling out of control. I have this picture in my mind of Steve trying to set up a sponsorship deal with let's say Virgin Airlines, and Richard Branson throwing down a picture from the Observer of a thousand Cardiff fans on the pitch or climbing over fences to get at rival fans, whilst wearing club shirts with "Fly Virgin" emblazoned over the front. Fuck me that would have been good business, who said no publicity was bad publicity?

The Rise and Fall of the Cardiff City Valley Rams

There was a story doing the rounds that the Kray twins once tried to buy the club, but dropped out when they were told that we could harm their reputation!

Other than Steve, most chairmen when having to deal with the fans would try and use the big stick approach; Sam Hamman on his arrival took a totally different approach. Sam used in his words the "you got to meet them to beat them" approach.

I am sure we played our part at the Rams and so did the supporters club through the work that Vince Alm put in, but at the end of the day Sam took a unique approach to solving the age old problem.

Many people ridiculed and slated this approach; Sam was seen by some as little more than a hooligan himself. The council, the police, the business community told him to step back and change his approach or he'd have no support from these sections (not that they'd given us anyway).

Most of us remember the hidden camera set up that followed Sam around on some of his visits to places such as the darkest quarter of Porth in the Rhondda, or other venues where he would go to try and get his message out there.

The famous incident after the Leeds game when we the club and its fans were being hung out to dry, Sam addressed around 100 of us at the club in the John Charles suite and told us that we were all in it together. If we wanted to be known as the biggest small club with the hooligan fans, then carry on, if we wanted to be playing top teams week in week out like Leeds (oh, how times change) then we would have to play our part. It was all positive anti hooligan stuff. Yet the only thing this hidden camera exposed and which they decided to show was a throw away jokey comment, which made us and Sam look even worse than the image 99% of the British population already viewed us with. Who can ever forget those pictures of the poor Leeds choir boys with such a blemish free reputation? Battered and bleeding from the vicious assaults at the hands of the Cardiff thugs, whilst in truth the only injuries they suffered that night (other than to their pride, and hard hooligan image) were from police batons and police dogs who were forced to use them to keep order, or when their clothes got ripped trying to climb over the fences.

Yes, whilst we can't bury our heads in the sand we'd have to admit that if police hadn't put a line in front of the Grange End fence and kept the Cardiff fans at bay, there would have been carnage. But the police did a great job that night and whilst there were thousands on that pitch who would have loved a full on ruck with the Leeds fans, it must be stated that the vast majority of them had gone on the pitch at the end of the game simply to celebrate. We were a mid table first division team, and we had just knocked Leeds United, the top team in the English Premiership out of the cup. What most reports and camera footage failed to highlight, was the scores of Leeds fans up on the fence at the front of the Grange End giving it the big one, calling it on, spitting and throwing coins. Fuck me, Sam was painted as the villain of the peace, yet before the match started, Sam had walked around the pitch side with a banner saying "Cardiff city welcomes Leeds United fans" and spent the whole walk in front of the Leeds fans dodging, pies, spit,coins and racist chants.

When the Leeds fans were finally let out of the stadium to get on their coaches, they themselves had charged at the temporary fences and knocked several over, forcing the police to drive them back. Perhaps they should have let them get through and saved themselves the trouble of battering them, because there were a few thousand Cardiff fans who were more than up for the job and were just waiting for the chance.

Anyway, in the world's eyes the damage had been done, you'd swear we'd shot Father Christmas, even people who hadn't heard of us hated us. What is it Millwall say "no one likes us, we don't care?" Well the world and his dog hated us that night, (mind you I'm sure there were a few Man United fans, Leeds United's arch enemies who picked Cardiff as their second club after that night, lol)

Now, whilst we felt as Cardiff fans, we were being treated unfairly or at the very least a bit heavy handed for that nights events, we had to hold our hands up and accept that we were paying the price for our years of "badness" whilst floundering in the wilderness of the lower reaches of the Football League and running roughshod up and down the country.

However, after that night what we did do was close ranks and pull together. We had formed the Valley Rams by this stage and were just getting established; however we never wanted to be seen or even be part of the "establishment". The majority of our members would avoid authority or establishment like the plague. Yet in truth to get things sorted we needed a different approach than the "fuck them all attitude" that we had got by on in the past.

When I got home that night I couldn't get to sleep. My mind was racing, I was feeling a responsibility that I had never felt before, and I don't think I was on my own. What Sam had managed to do was instil in some of us, the message that we had to be responsible for our own actions. It was our club and we were harming it and holding it back from future development.

This feeling of personal responsibility had bitten into me, and many times in the future it would bite me and many others again and again. I thought back to the week previous when we had played Bristol City at Ninian Park. Now if truth be told there was more trouble that day than at the Leeds match. Even now to many of us, we see Bristol City as our main rivals, even in comparison to Swansea. A lot of that depends on your age, but when I was growing up and the Hooligan period was at its peak, we played Bristol City on a regular basis, and unlike a trip to Swansea, Bristol was in another country and we had to cross water to get there (even if it is only a wide river). So the rivalry/hatred was well ingrained. Now, prior to the Bristol game we had meetings with the police regarding a better understanding of each others' needs and problems and had started trying to work together.

One of the major problem areas was taking place week in week out on Sloper Road. What the police used to do was put two lines across the road (and there's only one road that we all have to come out onto) these Police lines would form up and lot's of fair minded law abiding football fans would be stuck behind these lines unable to move through either side to get to their cars or coaches, they would be forced to wait there until they let out the away fans who would have to cross this road to get to their car and coach park.

Now, on the rare occasions, when away fans would dare to venture to the "third world hell hole" that we called home, a lot of our "lads" would congregate behind these police lines, or hang about in the car park. I can't begin to justify this, especially as I would be there myself on many occasions. Why was I there? Why was anyone there? Why didn't we all just go straight home?

Well there are many various reasons and not all of them apply to me. I would stay behind sometimes out of possibly a morbid curiosity, why was it?

In my school days as it was for so many I'm sure, we'd be hanging around the yard at lunchtime and the shout "fight" would go up, every man and his dog would want to see this fight. Why should it interest so many of us to possibly witness a fight where either it gets broken up by older lads or teachers, or it can involve one slap and be over with, or you may witness a real beating when one of the two lads gets the upper hand, often one lad would be hurt, more by the humiliation of losing or having to "give up" than the physical damage, why the urge to witness that, which of those options should interest any of us, but they always did, I can only speak on my experiences at these occasions, but I am sure there are a few of you reading this who have been there and seen it as well.

Now back to the football and the "gathering of the lads" that I referred to.

These lads were a real mix; you would have the young wannabes who thought it would give them street cred to stand amongst the older lads, act tough, chuck the occasional brick or stone (which in most case would end up hitting their fellow Cardiff fans on the back of the head.

It was mental. The old car park was just rough ground and there were stones everywhere. An endless supply of ammo for the stone chuckers. I was surprised that Billy Badge (our resident, ticket tout and badge selling entrepreneur) hadn't set up a stall in the car park selling perfect size throwing stones, hand picked by local virgins.

Then you had the slightly older ones who may have actually got stuck in, if they saw Cardiff getting the upper hand, but they'd have been on their toes if any genuine away lads had broken through (remember Hull on that night match?). Then you had the real "nutters" who would have loved a full scale tear up and would have been bang at it until arrested, knocked out or victorious with the away fans in retreat.

Then there were the older heads, those that had come through all this in their early days, but were still up for it. These didn't want to be seen as "hooligans" but at the first sign of trouble would have been stuck right into it. These older ones wouldn't be gesturing or throwing stones, just hovering in the background ready for back up if need be. It was and still is seen by many as defending your patch and your reputation for that matter. Childish, I know but better, more educated people than me have written loads on the reasons behind such things so I don't pretend to have the answers or reasons for it.

The last group could often contain much older people, some with their kids or even grandkids. They would wait by their cars looking with a morbid curiosity but with the chance to jump in their cars and feel safe if things got a bit too naughty.

All this would be taking place whilst thousands of your normal fans who really didn't fit into any of the above categories, but couldn't get anywhere because the police lines had blocked the road.

Now what used to happen was at a set time the police would push forward in both directions up and down the road and through the car park, in an effort to try and clear off the "risk element fans" as they call them. What would inevitably happen though on so many occasions was the "normal people" would get pushed by a copper, hit by a baton or even knocked out of the way by a 20 foot high horse (bit of an exaggeration I know, but fuck me have you ever stood next to one).

It used to be pandemonium and at the time there seemed to be no solution, but after a bit of team work and a new approach by the latest Police Officers who had been put in place at Cardiff games, things were soon to change for the better and quite rapidly.

Now back to the Bristol game, we had been told that Sky and lots of other media companies were coming down and setting up outside the ground, looking for some juicy stories and yet more bad publicity for our club.

A lot of us were concerned that any more problems could lead to the council refusing us the go ahead for the new stadium. Everything was in a delicate stage. Unfortunately, we didn't know what was yet to come with Leeds the following week, but first it was Bristol City and the problems that could bring with it.

We had held a Rams meeting that Thursday before the game, where we had over a hundred fans present, we discussed the possibility of the bad publicity that might come our way and suggested that some of our older more well known faces could play a part in helping.

One of the things we had suggested at the meetings with the police and the club, was rather than just let the police clear the road, we could have a line of our club stewards in between the police and our fans, these could act as a buffer and try and convince those hanging about to head home, also the club tannoy could announce that the CCTV cameras were watching everyone in the road and just reminding them that they were being filmed.

Now on the day in question the game had finished and Bristol City were locked in the ground. The normal baying mobs had gathered and so had the TV crews looking for some great footage of the inevitable chaos that they were hoping for.

The tannoy was belting out the message to leave the road and how it would bring trouble on the club etc. Now in all fairness, some people did start leaving the scene, but there were still large mobs in the main flashpoint areas. The stewards formed a line and tried to move forward speaking sense to the lads and again some listened and moved away, but there was one gang of youngsters, whose average age was around 18, bouncing around giving it the big one.

Some of these were throwing shadow punches and kicks at the stewards without really making contact, but more than likely the nearest they'd ever been to an actual fight. I could see the stewards were a bit uncomfortable with this. They weren't paid to have to scrap with fans in the road outside the ground, and fuck me they were only earning £25 or so a game, hardly worth getting a kicking for. The majority of our stewards were fans who wanted to help out the club. They could see the game for nothing and get a couple of quid for their troubles.

I could see the police clocking this situation and were just about to move through the stewards and resort to driving everyone up the road, which would then lead to the very situation we wanted to avoid. I had a rush of blood and jumped in this gap between our stewards and these youngsters. I tried to reason with the lads at the front. I was shouting "look boys you ain't going to get anywhere near the Bristol fans. You're all getting picked up by the CCTV cameras and worse of all, your going to fuck up our chances of getting a new stadium". Well in all fairness I could see some of them were taking it on board. Some of the older heads mixed amongst them, knew me and knew where I was coming from, but suddenly this one lad fronted me and said "fuck your stadium" and it just struck a chord with me. I thought yes "my stadium" and I don't mean my stadium personally, but what it did show me was this lad didn't give a flying fuck whether or not we had a new stadium or not, nothing any of us said would stop him from doing his best to mess things up, so I just gave him a good bitch slap. His eyes were spinning, I was half expecting to get piled on by all his mates, but most stepped back, one started to get a bit lippy and I grabbed him around the throat and I could see the colour draining from him, job done!

They turned around and as expected started a bit of the brave verbals when they were a safe distance away. But the job had been done. Whilst all this was happening a couple of Valley Rams and other City fans that knew me, had come forward to back me up. So by now there was a half a dozen or so of us there, Bonehead from Blackwood was one, and Dean from Brynthcethin who was a real good lad and a Rams Rep taking the bookings and running the coaches from that area. Dean died tragically less than a couple of years later and it was a really sad time for so many of us. He was a real diamond and funnily enough he was there by my side in Coventry a few months later for an evening cup match, when there was another bit of trouble to sort out, but this time with it was with rival fans rather than some of our own so called fans.

I was hoping that the TV cameras hadn't clocked what had happened and also half expected a tug by the police, but neither happened. However a lot of the club stewards came up and thanked me and it did put a bit of a line in the sand so to speak. It wasn't done as a big heroic thing, fuck me I'm 6ft 6" 20 stone and this lad was half my size and the same age as the shoes I had on. It was just a bit of a turning point and luckily those days of chaos outside the ground on Sloper road are more or less condemned to the past.

The car park is now covered in tarmac and there are no stones to use as ammunition any longer. The police now have a different method of letting people pass up and down the road for a good period after the game. This means that those who want to get away and back to their cars and coaches can do so. If it is a "risk game" and the away team have brought some numbers who are up for it so to speak, the police keep them in for ten minutes or so, giving the road a chance to clear, so that by now anyone hanging around is usually hanging around for a bit of nonsense, but now they are far more isolated and easier to pick out. They can then be moved away without loads of innocents getting caught up in things before the away fans are let out to cross the road and get on they're coaches, or to be bubbled up and escorted back to the station.

In fact things have moved on so much now that in the vast majority of cases, the away fans are let out at the same time as the Cardiff fans and simply cross the road in and amongst the city fans, don't get me wrong there are always large numbers of police around this spot and if there are any little square ups, they are in there like a flash but it is far smoother now than it's ever been.

I think even our maddest of mad fan now realises the pointlessness of hanging around outside the ground after the game. Nothing is going to happen. It doesn't impress the away fans. In fact in my opinion it makes us look childish. I feel we have grown up now from thinking it's big and brave to flash the V or give cut throat signs or stand there with your arms outstretched calling it on and shouting come on then (what the fuck is all that all about anyway?)

It cracks me up when you see a rival fan, 50 yards away, behind 3 rows of different fences and two rows of coppers, giving you the outstretched come on signals, and then when you don't instantly climb over the fences and beat your way through the coppers, whilst being filmed on CCTV. Because you fail to do this, does it mean you're scared of him? He's harder than you and he can go home head held high and proud that he's done a job on you? For fuck sake "get real"!

And as for throwing stones, well you got to be a real hard man to throw stones!

I have been in the car park and seen young wannabes, standing there in their bright orange luminous jackets, bend down, pick up a stone, then (and here comes the clever bit) they put their scarf over their face (so they can't be recognised when they throw the stone) they throw the stone and then pull their scarf back down and think they've been really hard, really clever and got away with it. Then Monday morning they have a knock on the door, Old bill "Ask Mummy is your son Johnny at home?" In they go, show the video and he says "That ain't me in the luminous orange jacket; it must have been someone else". Fucking genius!

I've often thought that if they connected a few of those red dot efforts they use on gun sites to some of the CCTV cameras, fuck me that would spook you. Can you imagine you're there with a brick in your hand or the old arms outstretched routine and suddenly there's a red dot on your forehead?

Another thing I thought would be a great laugh, and I have even suggested this to Nashy the stadium manager at Ninian Park. In the Grangend each side of the segregation area between home and away fans. When each group look across at each other they see a fence about shoulder height, and then all the heads and shoulders of the rival fans above this.

Now I thought it would be great if on these fences you could paint or run a full length banner showing the old seaside type picture of fat ladies in polka dot bathing costumes, and skinny old men in their trunks holding a beach ball, or even clowns with big shoes and spotted clothes, or babies in nappies etc. Now these pictures could have the heads taken off them, and then when the rival fans come up to the fence mouthing off and gesturing to the rival fans, all they see at each side would be these stupid characters, with wannabe's heads above each one, it would be funny as fuck!

I don't want to be seen to dismiss the present level of so called "hooliganism" as if it doesn't exist. The problem is a lot of the youngsters involved are playing a game totally out of their league so to speak. The problem is when it does come on top as it did at Spurs, you had hundreds of younger kids who couldn't work out why the rival fans weren't running away from them and actually wanted a full on tear up, you could see the kids thinking "oh Fuck this isn't how it's supposed to work out" I for one was glad to see so many of them have such a wake up call, luckily for them there were hundreds or more like thousands of older blokes who knew what to expect and were more than ready for it. It was a mad night at Spurs that night and in "hooligan terms" the honours were even. Basically meaning both groups involved made a good show and both parties saved face. At the time Spurs had for this period risen to the top few of the Hooligan league table, they had become very active over the recent years once again, and this game against Cardiff was seen as the top of the bill prize fight of the Century.

This one game must have tested the Met's football policing to the full. The week before the game took place, during our meetings and on the various message boards I had been trying to get the message out to our fans, stick together, don't take liberties and be on your guard.

Well that message went over everyone's head because as soon as each bus arrived at Spurs the 50 lads on board would be off looking for the first pub they could find. This is something that happens week in week out with very few problems, but this wasn't your bog standard game against Norwich or Torquay, this was Spurs and only one stage down from a war zone. It was rumoured that Kate Adie was asked to cover the game for BBC News and cried off saying she was safer in Iraq.

Well back to the first line of the book and Mog's shouting down my phone for back up. He was just one of many that night in a pub with a bunch of mixed fans. Lots of families, normal every day fans and 20 or 30 lads, who were up for anything. Next thing a scaffold pole comes through the window and there are 200 Spurs lads attacking the pub with enough stuff to fill two skips. This story was being repeated in half a dozen or so pubs around Spurs that night, luckily no one from either group were badly hurt. I was getting calls from several lads telling me to get some boys down to such and such pub and for a while it was mayhem.

After the game you had the situation of 4,000 Cardiff fans being let out of the stadium en masse, it was awesome and very powerful, the police were everywhere but they were stretched, there were several flash points and one occasion by the fenced off tennis courts it looked likely for a few minutes that our lads could break through and get at Spurs. If that fence had gone down, there would have been an unstoppable full on riot. The fence did its job however and the honours even awards were handed out. But being biased obviously, I am sure if a massed mob of 4,000 of our fans had got amongst Spurs that night there would have been only one outcome.

Events such as Spurs will pop up now and then and need policing accordingly, but you didn't need police intelligence to tell you that game had potential written all over it.

However the problems usually occur when people least expect it and are caught on the hop. One story sent to me by one of our older heads Andy (Pitbull) sums up such a situation. He was part of a small group of our older more able lads returning home from a uneventful game at Crewe, they had gone up by train for this one and the situation the got caught up in, is one most of us older heads have come across at some time or other without looking to hard.

Cardiff had just played Crewe in the final game of the season and about 15 of us caught the train back. Most of the city fans that went by train caught a different train as ours was going via Bristol Parkway. On the train back we opened our cans and played cards just a normal day back from the football, or so we thought.

Just outside the station the tannoy announced we are about to arrive at Cheltenham, I said to a few of the lads we might see the odd Rovers fan here, what an understatement. Little did we realise what was waiting for us. As we pulled into the station the platform was packed for its whole length with Bristol Rovers fans.

A couple of young city fans started to panic as Rovers were banging the windows and giving us the usual abuse, cut throat gestures and wanker signs. Someone shouted at the youngsters to get under the tables, some normal passengers started to crawl under the tables as well. About 10 of us made our way out of the carriage to the door we were determined not to let Rovers get into the carriage as we would have been slaughtered.

The train door opened and on they came, but seeing us they wouldn't venture any further than a foot inside the door. We were screaming at them and they were screaming at us. The ones at the back of their mob were pushing forward but the ones at the front wouldn't move any further as they knew the first ones in would have been battered.

It was like a scene from the film 300 Spartans with us massively outnumbered but in such a small space we couldn't be dislodged. Missiles were being chucked at us including a Walls ice cream sign, which we stupidly threw back about three times. Every time we threw it, the bastard thing came straight back at us. It always hit one of us as we were so close together.

One of their lot in the front started to get a bit braver and was getting closer and closer so I lunged forward and grabbed his jumper and pulled it over his

The Rise and Fall of the Cardiff City Valley Rams

head, I dragged him on the floor and held him down and was screaming at the lads to hit him. About 3 boys just kicked the living shit of him. He was out cold, so I let him go and the Rovers fans pulled him by his feet out of the train with his head bumping on the step and the platform. Rovers kept coming and with the weight of numbers we got forced back into the carriage.

This was bad news for the Rovers at the front of their mob as they were jammed in the space we had just defended. They couldn't go back and couldn't swing punches as they were being crushed by the numbers behind them. The three of us in the front were hitting the shit out of them, cheers, to Big Sam and the Mad Irishman. The Cardiff lads behind us were throwing punches over our shoulders and these Rovers in front took a right hammering. They then started to leave and someone shouted they could hear sirens.

It was then I looked round the carriage, what a sight, every window was put through, there was a bench hanging from a window, there was blood everywhere as one of the lads had been hit in the face with an unopened can and had a hell of a cut. There were people appearing from under tables and there was my old mate the Walls ice cream sign!

Outside, I noticed a few Rovers lads still on the platform so I jumped up on the seat and started kicking the window, which was already smashed, until there was a couple of big holes in it. Terry then put a fire extinguisher nozzle through the window hole and just as he was about to fire it at the Rover's fans they pushed the nozzle through the second hole Bang, he fires it and gets fucking sprayed with foam, ha ha.

Whilst this was all going off I kept thinking what if Rovers come through the carriage and get behind us. What I didn't realise was that there was fighting at three different train doors, Steve had fought a lone battle with the fire extinguisher as a weapon. We were on another and the Caldicot boys were at another. One of the Caldicot boys was pretty badly banged up and one of his teeth was knocked out. When he was taken for treatment just outside the station the Rovers mob tried to get at him in the first aid room.

When we stepped onto the platform there was debris everywhere and the place looked like a Swansea council estate. Plod told us that a new train was coming as this one wasn't fit for humans. We thought some of us might get nicked but a copper said they knew it was self defence as a Japanese tourist had filmed everything and they'd viewed the footage. If you're that Jap and your reading this I wouldn't mind buying a copy.

After about an hour another train arrived and we were put in one carriage with plod guarding the door, the rovers had the rest of the train. It was only then I realised that there was only 22 of us.

One funny note to the story, when we got back to Parkway we got off and about 40 rovers got off as well. When they were going through the car park opposite the platform they were giving us all the usual abuse. One of them stayed too long and hadn't seen the police dog rushing towards him off the leash, the dog started ripping fuck out of him until his handler arrived and pulled him off.
    ANDY

Chapter 2
The Leeds aftermath

We, the fans and the club realised after the Leeds game that something had to change. These changes couldn't and wouldn't happen overnight, but as with any challenge, taking the first step was often the hardest.

After the meeting in the John Charles suite when the TV cameras had stitched us up, a lot of us went home that night, angry at what we felt was the unfair press we were attracting, and what could we do to turn things around. We had hit rock bottom and now we had to get back up.

That night I was lying in bed with the cogs whirring around in my head and one of the things I came up with was the "Fans Charter" My plan was to get a name for this charter, get a petition going, get people involved and get some publicity. The press and media involved with football related events on and off the pitch were all new to me. Like many others, I used to believe that what I read in the papers, seen on the television, or heard on the radio was the truth, otherwise how could it be broadcast.

I was taking my first steps on a massive learning curve. I had watched Sam dealing with and manipulating the press and was picking up little pointers. I remember him saying that he could tell what type of direction a particular article would take just by looking at the photograph linked to it.

Now I thought when they printed a story that Sam was heavily involved in, that they would take a current photo and link that to the story, but how it works is they have banks and banks of photos and footage on file. So if the story relates to Sam having a battle with the Council or FA for example, you will see a scowling frowning picture and vice versa if it's an up beat story.

This was never truer than when they came to show the expose on our club, it started off showing the approach to Ninian Park on a real dark gloomy looking evening. My God, I thought I was about to watch a re-showing of "Hitchcock's" film Psycho.

Also I learnt that when the press would interview you, they would have an agenda or at the least a vision of how they wanted the story to pan out. Therefore, whatever you said, they would try and lift the slightest quote or phrase you used and place it out of context to benefit the story they wanted to get out. Often you would do a ten minute interview and they would use a five second snippet that was totally irrelevant to the message you were trying to get out there.

The Rise and Fall of the Cardiff City Valley Rams

One such example that taught me a lesson was during the period when Lennie Lawrence was the club manager. The teams form was erratic to say the least. My mate Sam Murphy hit the nail on the head when he said in one newspaper interview, that the best team and the worse team he had seen that season were Cardiff City. One week we could beat a team who were flying high four nil away from home, then lose two nil at home to a team languishing at the bottom of the table. None of us new what team was taking the pitch from one week to the next, not that the playing staff would change, just that their attitude and approach would? Now whilst the fans were getting frustrated and annoyed, the manager must have been going mental.

Anyway, the press must have thought it would be "good press" to get Lennie out" so they would interview certain fans leaders etc. for comments.

My interview went along the lines of, I felt the players should take a long hard look at themselves, we had heard there was a lot of little cliques in the changing rooms and player power issues. Changing the manager may not achieve the long term results we wanted. However, when a club did change a manager, the first 5 or 6 performances usually improved, because all the players would be trying to impress the new manager, this was usually only a short term solution. So in my opinion it was in the players hands, we knew they could play and felt they should be doing that regardless of who the manager was. I added lots of other bumf as well, yet the only part they used under the title of "Gwyn Davies, the head of the Valley Rams supporters club states" that if the team replaced Lennie Lawrence and got a new manger in, then the performances would improve. It really stitched me up. When I spoke to Lennie and told him about the article, he wasn't the slightest bit phased and was used to the crap the press would come up with. A sharp lesson for me and I ain't been caught too often since.

Anyway back to trying to get some positive press after the Leeds game, I spoke to Vince at the supporters club and Jinx and Corky my right hand men at the Rams. The plan was we'd set up this "Fans Charter" and call it **"SEE"** this would stand for Sam's, Eyes & Ears. It took the form of a petition and we printed off sheets and got almost ten thousand signatures within the first week.

The heading of this petition read, "We the undersigned pledge our support to the S.E.E. Campaign, we the fans were no longer prepared to stand back and do nothing when other idiots were bringing shame and disrespect to our club". It went on to say that we would act as Sam's eyes and ears and that if we saw or witnessed any disorder such as throwing objects on the pitch, or someone climbing a fence to get on the pitch, we would either take action ourselves, or at the very least draw it to a steward's attention. Also if we heard racist chanting or abuse the same would apply.

Now this was quite heady stuff and we were walking a fine line. To be seen or thought of as a "Grass" was up there with child molesting or wife beating.

The thought to many of us that we would or should dob someone in was foreign to our beliefs. Therefore the approach we took was that anyone who was prepared to damage the club's image and our whole future would be seen as the enemy and we the fans could not let the enemy destroy our club. All sounds a bit corny and idealistic now but the press loved it. And in fact it did achieve it's goals to some extent and on some occasions if (as was usually the case) some young knob-head who came to a game once a year would go to throw a coin or something at the ref or opposing player, a fan or fans would collar him and wise him up. I'd like to think that the fans did see the sense in this and also no longer felt isolated and that other decent minded fans would back them up.

We really have seen a massive reduction in any incidences since those days and I for one genuinely can't remember an incident taking place or being reported since. Now I don't for one minute think that the Charter cured this problem solely. The improved CCTV, better policing and stewarding were all a part of this, but the fans had, and still are playing their part. In fact this has led to all the fences being now taken down at Ninian Park, something I thought I'd never see in the peak of the madness. I do feel a sense of pride with this, but no more than any other fan should, because everyone has played a part in this. We did turn things around and we did get permission for the new stadium, because it did look at the time as if no one in power would touch us with a barge pole.

The last thing as a fan that I want to see at Ninian Park however is the "Prawn Sarnie" image. The day that happens is the day I, and many others I feel will pack our bags and leave. Yes we can't have hooligans and disorder, but we can still make it hostile and intimidating without breaking any laws.

A packed house all getting behind the team is worth a goal start, and if you can get under the opposing teams skin, then great. You don't have to climb on the pitch or chuck objects to do that, just sheer volume and passion is often enough.

I remember the build up to the Leeds match. David O'Leary the team manager told the Leeds team to close all the curtains on the coach and told the players to keep their heads down for the last 3 or 4 miles as they approached the stadium. Fuck me; he almost did our job for us! The players must have been crapping themselves before they even got on the pitch.

I'm sure I don't need to remind people of the score or again of the events that happened or supposedly happened that night. However, after the game had finished Stuart Cable (who was the drummer with the Stereophonics at that time) and Kelly Jones the lead singer, happened to be in the reception area of the club when Robbie Fowler (who had played for Leeds that night) spotted Stuart Cable. They had met before and were quite friendly. Robbie called Stuart over for a chat, and later that evening back in Cwmaman working men's club Stuart and Kelly told me the story of what he'd said.

Apparently he'd told them that he couldn't wait to get off the pitch. He said it was like a zoo out there and the most scared he'd ever been in his life. Stuart had supposedly said to him "For fuck sake Robbie, I thought you were born in Toxteth and be used to all that" and Robbie replied that it was the scariest place he'd ever been to and he hoped he'd never have to come back here again. Ironic really when you considered he signed and spent a season with us 2007-2008.

As stated earlier the press and media were hanging us out to dry. They were calling for an FA enquiry which duly came about.

The FA whilst finding incidents such as coin throwing had taken place, they also had to accept that it had come from both sets of fans, and whilst Cardiff City had to accept some of the blame, there's not a lot a club can do to stop people entering a ground with loose change in their pockets. The FA however made several suggestions regarding measures they'd like to see implemented regarding CCTV and segregation netting etc. and our club set about carrying out these tasks.

Now what the baying public and press needed to remember was that we weren't the only club ever to have coins thrown on the pitch. We weren't the only fans to run on the pitch after a game to celebrate a famous victory, and if they were heavy handed with our punishment then at the very least they would have to be consistent and impose any such punishments on any clubs taking such actions in the future.

On the night in question, one Radio broadcaster had managed to get in and interview Sam Hamman, now Sam was well used to journalists with agenda's, but apparently this one was bang out of order and it ended with Sam's minder Macca turfing the knob-head out into the car park. Now I can't remember if this broadcaster was from Five live or Talk Sport, but either way his bosses weren't too happy with our club (not that anyone was at that time. lol) Every chance that channel had they'd stick the knife into us first opportunity.

This culminated in one show a week or so later devoting almost it's entire phone in slot of around an hour on a Friday afternoon, to slate the FA for only fining us a few thousand pounds. The presenter was calling for us to be thrown out of the league and our homes burnt to the ground (well almost).

He was asking for people to phone in and give their views, now in radio terms this means phone in and agree with my views and agenda and we'll get you straight on, phone in with a different view and we'll pretend to keep you on hold in a queue and the apologise for not being able to get your call aired.

I was driving down the M4 in Newport at the time of listening to this and the hairs on the back of my neck were bristling, I was trying to think on my feet (or on my arse this time because I was driving) So I phoned in and spoke to the call handler and said that I was the Spokesperson for the Valley Rams who were one of the two Official supporters groups at Cardiff City.

I told him that I agreed that the fine was derisory and that we should have had a much heavier punishment.

I could feel this bloke punching the air with excitement "yes we even have a Cardiff fan agreeing with us now" Fuck me surprisingly they managed to get me straight on as the next caller. Now the presenter was one of the well known ones either Durham or Littlejohn if I'm not mistaken, but he fucking hated us. He opened up by saying "and we have Gwyn Davies on the line", he gave my title on line and the big build up and then said "finally we have a Cardiff fan that agrees with us, about this pitiful fine".

Bang I was straight in, "yes" I said "it's derisory, we should have been fined much more or at very least be thrown out of the competition" I could sense this bloke coming in his pants. I said "who do we think we are at Cardiff, we are a mediocre second division team based in Wales, and we had the audacity to knock out the mighty Leeds United, who were Premiership leaders and former European champions".

I had him, but he came straight back with "but what about the coin throwing incidents" and I said "yes but the Leeds fans were frustrated and did that out of frustration, I can't condone it but it does happen week in week out in the Premiership" now he said "What about the coins thrown on by the Cardiff hooligans" I replied "oh, I'm sorry I thought the FA had found both sets of fans guilty of throwing coins on the pitch, I thought that included the well behaved Leeds football supporters and not just the Cardiff hooligans". He started stuttering a bit now trying to come back at me, "well what about that pitch invasion at the end of the game" well on the same weekend we had played Leeds, Man United had Villa at Villa Park. I can't remember the score but I think Man U had gone 2-1 down when suddenly Man U scored and Alex Ferguson jumped on the pitch side punching the air, some Man U fans also spilled onto the pitch, one minute later they scored what turned out to be the winning goal. Alex Ferguson was back on doing a jig and this time a load more Man U fans got on the side of the pitch jumping with joy.

So I went back at him and recounted this Man United incident that half the country had witnessed on national TV, he came back at me and said "well Man United had just scored and they were simply celebrating" daft twat. I had him by the bollocks now, "oh, I said when Man United fans run on the pitch and celebrate a victory, that's okay, when Cardiff city fans who have just knocked the best team in England out of the cup and run on the pitch "after the game had finished incidentally" then that's not okay and classed as a riot?"

He was fucking floundering now. "Well what about those Welsh songs they were playing over the tannoy to incite trouble and that Sam Hamman standing behind the goal inciting the fans to riot". Again I replied "If you had ever watched a Cardiff game, you'd know that for the second half of every game, Sam stands there behind the goal" and as for the Welsh song inciting riots, is that because you simply don't understand the words and automatically think the worse. It's our tradition and heritage, just as Walk alone is the tradition and heritage at Anfield" I said "It all sounds a bit racist and sounds as if you have a hatred of all things Welsh". Well he couldn't wait to get me off the air now; he'd shown himself in his true colours and looked like a complete prat. Within seconds I was getting loads of calls from City fans, chuffed as fuck that someone had got through and had a say, we were all frustrated, yes things had happened that were out of order, but no worse than what was happening week in week out all around the country.

The best call came off Steve Borley, he said "well done Gwyn you fucking mullered him"

Scott Young with some of the Valley Rams (Ant Hill crew)

Mathew and some of the Bridgend Valley Rams

Chapter 3
Top of Form
The Huddersfield trilogy

Prior to 2001, Huddersfield Town was a team we'd come up against on and off throughout previous seasons but with no real history of trouble and no bad blood as such between the fans. Actually, even now there is no bad blood as such between both sets of fans but sadly for a lot of Cardiff fans the mention of Huddersfield police will bring a reaction of disgust bordering on hatred.

This has come about from the three visits we had made to Huddersfield Town between 2001 and 2003. Two of visits were in one season when one match was called off and had to be replayed later on in the year and then the following seasons match made up our third visit.

To a lot of us the experience of dealing with the police at Huddersfield epitomises everything that is wrong and bad about policing at football in England. I hope to enlighten on some reasons behind that opinion during this next chapter.

The first visit in question was I believe a Tuesday night match scheduled for January. I had gone up in one of two early coaches that the Rams had booked. We had gone up early for a couple of reasons: - one was because of the distance involved; we wanted to make a day of it and have an afternoon in a pub for a drink and a meal. Also, because of complications with the bus drivers tachos, rather than have 2 drivers per bus, it meant you either had to go straight up and straight back for the drivers to be within their hours. Or in the case we chose, to get up there early enough so that the drivers could park up and to have a minimum of a 5 hour break.

There was nothing sinister about us going up early, we had told the South Wales police of our plans and we had built up enough trust for them to know that we hadn't gone up looking for or planning trouble. When we arrived at Huddersfield which must have been around 3pm the drivers dropped us off in the town centre and they went off to park the coaches at the stadium. We made our way through the town and found a Weatherspoons pub. Cheap beer, cheap food, and all of us happy as pigs in shit. Whilst I said that we hadn't gone up planning trouble, I did have a moment flash by me whilst walking through the main street in Huddersfield and realising that the hundred or so of us in our group must have looked quite an intimidating sight. I think the youngest ones in our group would have been aged 30 plus. We had loads of characters with us, Ketty, Sam, Macca, Mogs, Joey Mullins and plenty of other faces who shall we say were well known.

We had been in Weatherspoons for 20 minutes or so before the first sign of any police. Two of them walked in, had a look around and whilst they could see that there were no signs of aggression, I could tell from their body language that they were well pissed off that we had got into the pub and slipped through their net so to speak.

From that moment on we were never without a police presence and at the minimum there were two van loads parked outside until later when we left.

Throughout the afternoon our numbers began to swell as small groups who had come up by car or train phoned mates to find out where we were and came to join us. A couple of these lads who were more "soul crew" minded shall we say, were popping in and out and came back with reports that "their pub" meaning the Huddersfield lads was only a few hundred yards around the corner.

These younger lads were trying to drum up support for us to leave en masse and head up to this other pub. But none of our lads were interested and the attitude was that if any of them have got a beef with us and want trouble let them come up here. It more or less sums up a lot of our boys' attitude. They wouldn't really cross the road looking for trouble but they would deal with any if it came looking for them. There was a real party mood in the pub, you could see that the police were getting edgy, but because there were no complaints within the pub and no problems, there was little that they could do about it.

The plan was at 7pm; we would all leave together and take the ten minute walk up to the stadium. Unfortunately, at around 6.45pm one of the lads had a phone call saying that the game had been called off because of a waterlogged pitch.

At first we thought that this was a piss take but within seconds we had several other calls confirming that the game was off. We were all totally cheesed off, but again there was no aggression, we were simply resigned to the fact that the game was off. It wasn't the first time and it wouldn't be the last. Most of us had the view that at least we had had a good swig all afternoon, whilst the majority that had come up on the other coaches were just getting there and now having to turn back and head for home.

The Police came in to the pub ten minutes later and announced to us that the game had been called off and that they had arranged for our two coaches to be brought over to the pub to collect us. Again, no problem to be honest we were happy that it would save us a walk. When the coaches arrived outside, it was almost as if someone had flicked a switch, the whole attitude of the police changed from being a bit twitchy into almost full riot control situation.

We were ordered out of the pub and anyone who didn't immediately jump to their feet and rush to the doors was given the normal push and shove to encourage them. When we got to the doors there was a full gauntlet of Robocop's wearing full body armour and their staffs drawn.

Confrontations started taking place when some of the lads leaving the pub tried to get on their bus, which was the second one rather than the first one in the queue, the Police's attitude was the first 50 get on the first bus and the second 50 get on the second bus etc.

It was absolute madness. The boys were having none of it. Their bags and their belonging were on one bus and that was the bus they intended going home on even if it took a full on scrap with the South Yorkshire storm troopers to achieve it.

Finally after what seemed an eternity of jostling, pushing and shoving and confrontation, everyone managed to get on their correct bus. This could have all been achieved in two minutes flat with no problems at all if they had left us to our own devices. The bus drivers were told in no uncertain terms not to stop anywhere on the route home and just to ensure that they followed this order, I kid you not we had a full police escort (involving helicopters at certain times) blocking off every junction, service station and turn off between Huddersfield and Ross on Wye, covering a journey of what must have been 200 miles.

It was totally over the top and uncalled for. There had been no arrests and not even one glass had been smashed all day. There you are, we don't pay for it, do we? Oh, I forgot, we do pay for it, don't we?

The rearranged game had now been planned for some time in April, I believe. And after the welcome we had had in Huddersfield last time there was no way I would put our lads in the same position again. What we decided to do this time, again because of the driver's tachos etc was to offer our fans two options.

One option was, going straight up and back on the bus. The other option was as previous, again going up early and making a day out of it. But what we decided to do this time was get the buses to drop us off in Manchester city centre, where we could have a good drink well away from South Yorkshire's finest.

This trip proved even more popular and we had 4 coach loads for this early option. The day went like clockwork (until we arrived by train in Huddersfield). We had spent the afternoon in one or two pubs in Manchester, again with no problem. We left in plenty of time to catch the train for the 30 minute journey or so over to Huddersfield. There were 3 or 4 transport police waiting for us at Manchester station and these travelled with us over to Huddersfield. These coppers were the salt of the earth, we had great banter with them and actually one of them was a female who I believed swapped telephone numbers with one of the Barry boys.

When we got to Huddersfield, the transport police came with us and one of them even mentioned to us to watch out for ourselves because the police at Huddersfield had a reputation for being really heavy handed.

We came out of the station and there was a row of a dozen steps or so down to the main road. At the bottom of these steps was nothing short of a small army waiting for us.

There was half a dozen police horses, and scores of policemen all dressed up in full riot gear with their staffs drawn. There was no communication, we were just left standing on these steps, but it was made quite apparent that we were going nowhere until they had told us. It was around this time that one of our lads Paul Thomas from Merthyr, came rushing up to me and said "Gwyn, watch yourself, I heard one of the coppers talking and he said when it kicks off, get the big fucker with the video camera". Because of the events that had taken place during the previous match, I had taken my small hand held video camera, again for two reasons, one for evidence gathering if anything did happen and another as a bit of protection for our boys.

We had seen occasions in the past where coppers become far less aggressive when they realised that their actions are being filmed. Anyway, even after hearing what Paul had said to me, whilst it did spook me slightly, I tried to make sure that the coppers could see we were filming them.

I hoped this would keep everything calm, but I couldn't have been more wrong. When they finally decided to move us off, orders were shouted at us as if we were convicts from a chain gang. We were marched off in a bubble formation, which for those unaware of such tactics, is a full circle of officers, where you are wrapped or bubbled up inside. We were moved down the hill, which was possibly half a mile from the ground, at a pace governed by the police, with police horses and officers on foot in front of you setting the pace. Unfortunately, for those at the back, if the officers at the front slowed down for any reason, the lads at the back of the bubble would get pushed and kicked in the back of the legs and told to keep moving, which was impossible because the ones at the front had stopped. This type of tactic isn't unique to South Yorkshire and seems ludicrous that they can't have communication from the front row of officers to the back row of officers.

We had only gone down the hill a hundred yards or so when we were brought to a total standstill. But this standstill happened to be outside the very same Huddersfield pub that I mentioned earlier. This is apparently where the hooligan element gathers and obviously well known to the Huddersfield police. Seeing 200 Cardiff fans brought to a standstill outside their pub was really winding up the Huddersfield fans inside who proceeded to chuck everything they could out through the windows. There was no danger to us.

The pub must have been about 50 yards away from us on the right hand side. But instead of moving us along away from this hotspot, the police seemed simply intent on keeping us there, as if to make the situation even worse. But none of our boys responded, again this group of 200 were mostly older heads who had seen and been through it all in terms of football related matters such as this, they new we were being set up by the police, anyone who had been mad enough to run at the pub would have been straight in the nick.

Because none of our boys responded, this seemed to antagonise the police even more and they now started pushing inwards from all sides of the bubble compressing the already well packed group. Now I was aware at this time that besides for this group who had been attached to us, who we found out were a specialist group for such occasions (possibly called the South Yorkshire storm troopers), but also on the fringes of the route were your everyday local

Huddersfield policemen shall we say. And I could see the look of bewilderment on their faces; even they didn't know what was supposed to be happening.

Pandemonium was breaking out. We couldn't move anywhere, yet we were still being pushed and shoved. The horses were brought in amongst us and people were getting hit over the heads with staffs, it would appear just for the fun of it. This went on for a few minutes.

It then seemed to calm down. The front row of police moved forward and the bubble was yet again in procession. People were looking at one another in total amazement. Some with blood running down their faces, others shouting at coppers at what's going on and what was all that about etc.

We must have gone another 100 yards or so down the road and yet another repeat performance. The front row of coppers stopped still, the ones at the back and sides simply pushed in closer and closer and stage 2 of the South Yorkshire welcome took place. It was at this time whilst I was still filming I could see one copper making a beeline for me, he tried to grab the camera out of my hand. I managed to knock his hand out of the way and then he tried to knock the camera out of my hand with his staff. I remember shouting at him at the time "This is going to make you look good when we watch it later". The lads around me saw what was going on, came around me, I'd like to think to prevent me from having a hiding. But in reality I think they were more interested in protecting the video camera (lol). It was shortly after this moment where I noticed a copper ten yards or so further down the road on his horse simply strike out at one of the boys straight across his head. I tried to get closer to get better footage of what was going on and saw that it was Peter Morgan who had been hit across the head. Peter had automatically jumped back and shouted at the copper "What the fuck was that for?", which simply led to the copper cracking him over the head a second time with the staff.

Peter then jumped up in defence and tried to pull the copper of his horse but as he did so 4 or 5 officers on foot just waded into him and battered him unconscious to the ground with their staffs. Ketty had seen this and he ran straight through the coppers and dived on Mogs's back to shield him taking a dozen or so blows in the process. I started to realise now that the footage I had on video camera could be very damning to the police to say the least and I wanted to take measures to protect the footage I had taken.

I took the film cassette out of the camera and I gave it to Donald from Barry and I gave the camera to one of the Aberdare boys telling them both to try and get them into the ground and give them to one of our club stewards for safekeeping. I won't labour the details too much further because a book can be written on its own about the events then and after Huddersfield. However, of the 15 Cardiff fans that were arrested that night, when they appeared in court, the judge on seeing the evidence which included the footage that I had gathered dismissed the case against all the Cardiff fans and went on to say that if members of the public had seen the evidence that he had seen, they would be shocked and horrified to see how our police force who are meant to protect the public and keep order could behave.

He even went on to say that he would be calling for the officers involved to go on trial for their actions. We were ecstatic. We actually thought we would get a bit of justice, only for 18 months later or so to find out that the Crown Prosecution Service would not be taking action due to insufficient evidence. I and others still feel to this day that this case must have gone to the highest political levels and the pressure had been put on to prevent justice being done.

The harm and damage that could have been done to an already under pressure police force could have caused ripples throughout the country and I still feel that that was the reason that the guilty officers weren't brought to book. However, one of the Aberdare lads, Russell Meak did take out a private civil action and was awarded £8,000 on the understanding that he settled out of court. He accepted this and none of us can blame him for that, especially when a year later Mogs who was involved in the worse incident of the day tried to take a similar action and at the very final stages was told by his solicitors in a supposedly no win no fee case that if he didn't win his case in court he would be liable for a minimum of £35,000 costs. Putting enough pressure on Peter that forced him to finally drop proceedings.

British justice at its best!

The next section I have included was sent to me by one of the lads arrested that night.

Huddersfield v Cardiff City (The SET-UP)

I arrived in Huddersfield the day before the game spending the night in a local hotel with my Girlfriend.

On the day of the match we went into town early for some lunch and a look around.

Not knowing the area too well we ended up in a pub called 'The Crescent'.

We had some food and a couple of pints and a chat with some of the locals.

(At no time was I aware that this was Huddersfield's pub).

After spending a couple of hours there we went for a walk around town ending up in the Gas Club some 600 Yds from the ground.

Again the locals were very friendly even to the point that I ended up playing cards with a few of them.

Time was ticking by and eventually we decided it was time to leave for the ground.

On leaving this club, we were held at the exit by Old Bill. The next thing I could hear was quite a lot of noise coming from a large group being escorted by large numbers of mounted police. As the group came nearer it was immediately apparent that not all was well – a number of individuals with bleeding head wounds!

At this point my girlfriend and I were pushed by old bill into this large group of lads and told to 'join the rest of them'. This group of lads turned out to be the Valley Rams.

Within seconds of joining this group, the roadway narrowed into more of a lane.

Consequently there was now much less room than there had been.

The result – a number of people including my girlfriend were now being squashed by these police horses. In trying to say to the coppers that there was a woman present I was told to 'SHUT UP YOU WELSH CUNT' whilst having that big White horse driven into me. My girlfriend fell on the floor. A couple of us picked her up and again I said that there was a woman present.

With that, that prick of a copper (name and number withheld) drove his horse into me standing on my foot. That's when I saw red and tried to pull the police man off his horse.

All hell let loose with me and a few others being arrested.

CONCERN – My only concern was for my girl friend who hadn't long come out of hospital. She was now on her own in a town almost 200 miles away from home.

But, she wasn't on her own, she was with the Valley Rams and was soon taken in and accepted as part of 'the family'

All night, while stuck in that fucking cell I tried to tell the police that she was recuperating from a serious illness but they didn't give a fuck. – SURPRISE SURPRISE!

Three RAMS in particular looked after her all night staying in town and trying to get me out until 3.00am. Many thanks to Mikey, Garry & Elliot from the Do a Deer crew who remain staunch friends to this day.

Unfortunately, Andrea is no longer with us – she passed away In Feb 2007 aged just 41. Whenever we went to away games we would always make a phone call and find out where the RAMS were because she knew if we were with The RAMS then we were safe. The only thing we weren't safe from were the police.

RIP Andrea – a great person and one of the boys.

The third part of the trilogy came at that next game. This was a Saturday game 2003 and we had decided unanimously to limit any risk of another stitch up and simply do a normal away trip, up and back. If you wanted to stop on route then stop well outside the area, if you were "sneaking a drink on board" make sure it was all off the bus and none hidden underneath for the return journey. We didn't want to give them any excuse to get at us. We were in legal proceedings against several of their officers and that wasn't going to endear us to them.

We had fourteen Rams coaches booked for this game and the supporters club and some independent groups had another 10 coaches booked, so a total of twenty four coaches and a few hundred others as always travelling by car or train, so somewhere in the region of two thousand making the trip.

We had been given a time slot to arrive at some motorway service station just outside Huddersfield. As the Rams coaches started pulling in, the Supporters club coaches who had been given an earlier time slot were just pulling out, this was quite normal and we were happy for the supporters' club coaches who contained mostly families to get there and get away before we turned up along with all the chaos we provided!

Again, no surprise an army of police were gathered there waiting, each bus was emptied and searched. Individuals were searched and photographed, nothing new to us and part of our regular away day out.

The Rhondda bus, with Ketty and Stickeys boys on board had an exceptionally ugly turn out this day, the best looking bloke on board would have passed for a Speilberg extra. They frightened me and most of them were my mates. They were taken off the bus, searched as we all were and then allowed to get back on the bus.

We were just about to finally be taken out in a convoy when chaos broke out. The Rhondda bus got pulled over and was surrounded by every copper available. Fuck me I thought, what have they done now?

The police got them all back off the bus yet again and some started searching the bus again whilst the others set about searching every one on board for a second time.

I managed to get myself off our bus after convincing one of the coppers that I was the organiser of the group. I approached the senior officer near their bus and asked what the problem was, only to be told that as the bus was pulling out, one of the lads sitting on board was seen to roll his bobble hat down and it actually was a balaclava.

Fucking hell all this chaos and delay was caused because a copper had seen a lad wearing a balaclava. Luckily they didn't find his double barrelled shotgun. Can you imagine if they'd charged him with wearing a balaclava,, the judge would have laughed them out of court. Actually when he found out it was one of the Rhondda boys, the judge may have commended him for taking precautions not to frighten any one who happened to glance at the bus on route.

When we finally got moving, the convoy was kept at a speed of twenty miles an hour. We were still at least five miles from Huddersfield and there was only fifteen minutes to the kick off. Finally we could se the floodlights, thank God we're almost there, but there was still some more ludicrous policing to come yet. As we got into the coach park area, the police started insisting that each bus, starting with the first one would drop off their passengers one bus at a time. Well that was ok if you were on the first bus, but the ones on the last bus soon worked out, at that rate they were going to miss at least fifteen minutes of the game.

The lads on board weren't having any of this. We had all stuck to the plans and played our part and yet the police still wanting to put obstacles in our way. My God we had been on our buses over five hours by now, we just wanted to see a football game, but the relevance of that seemed irrelevant to the police yet again.

Emergency doors were flying open and people were getting off every bus through any exit they could find. Chaos, yet again. The police were coming in from all angles as if the crown jewels were getting robbed.

Everyone was now seen by the police as law breaking criminals and fair game for a clout. This event, just about sums up the approach taken to football fans! Especially where Cardiff fans are concerned.

These were just ordinary blokes trying to get in on time to watch a football game. They weren't criminals, but because they hadn't totally complied to the crazy plans which weren't working and causing problems they were now seen as a major threat to the whole fabric of the law.

I cannot stand back and defend all our fans and make out they're all angels, they aren't. But why antagonise and cause problems, if there was no need.

As far as I was concerned limiting the possibility of problems, and keeping everything in check was the way forward. If trouble broke out, then it would have to be dealt with, but why look for problems if there were none there, it was almost as if our reputation meant yet again the police's approach was get the retaliation in first, and bully people by fear in to compliance. Well I can assure you it doesn't work when dealing with Cardiff fans, and will some of us have to get killed before they realise this?

Finally when the police worked out, that rather than try and get seven hundred fans back on fourteen coaches, it was easier just to let them make their way into the stadium and common sense prevailed.

There were no problems during the game but at the final whistle we left to make our way back to the coaches. There were twenty four coaches there in total, so close on twelve hundred fans making their way towards them for the return journey.

But as I got nearer, I became aware that problems were breaking out yet again. Now Just as the year before the police seemed to have this master plan that the first fifty people approaching the coaches should get on the first bus, and the second fifty on the next bus and so on until each bus was full and ready to leave. You couldn't make it up, it was like ethnic cleansing. You had fathers being forced on one bus and their kids being put on another.

Now this wasn't just happening to a bunch of no neck lads, whole families were getting caught up and people who had never raised their voice let alone been in trouble were suddenly getting hit by police staffs trying to force them on to buses. Alan Kerslake who is our clubs chief steward and a former police inspector himself, tried to intervene, and he got whacked as well for his trouble.

Again it finally got sorted when the police realised they had twelve hundred frustrated and angry people at almost riot stage. The police stood back a few dozen yards possibly to regroup (or have another major consultative meeting to take a risk assessment before planning the next stage of their operation, my arse) and whilst this was going on, all the fans got on their allocated coaches and were ready to leave. Fuck me it wasn't brain surgery.

I kid you not, but several years later, I was asked to give a fans view of football policing at Liverpool University. Dr Cliff Stott had set it up and there were close on three hundred police present from all over the UK who were involved in football policing.

I had to give a presentation on stage to this lot and whilst it was nerve racking, I had so much pent up frustration inside me I was determined to give it my best shot. My presentation went down well and lots of officers present spoke to me after, saying that lots of what I said made sense and hopefully it would lead to changes for the better (yeah ok) one of those that came up to me had been involved in the Huddersfield fiasco.

He told me that they had learnt a lot of lessons after the last Cardiff match and one of the reasons for the problems was their mindset, that it didn't matter which bus they put the fans on to get them out of there because they were all heading back to the same place. They hadn't given it a second thought that people may be travelling back to different areas, which was especially true in our case, or that people would have left their belongings on their allocated bus. Fuck me you would have thought they'd reinvented the wheel when they solved this particular problem. Well any progress is progress I suppose. Perhaps the next thing they may work out is, if you treat people aggressively, then usually they will respond aggressively, it ain't rocket science.

Chapter 4
The structure, or lack of it

We had 3 rules at the Valley Rams. The first rule was that when we got within ten miles or so of whichever ground we were travelling to, we would have to clear the bus compartment of any booze. This was dependant upon any feedback or info we'd had. If for instance it was the West Midlands, then it meant booze off the bus, hidden in a hedge for the return journey. If it was an area where the policing was a bit more relaxed then it would mean hiding the drink in the storage areas under the bus.

The second and third rules were _ _ _ _ _ _, that's right there were no second and third rules.

This was part of the psychology used at the start and very much needed if we were to attract the type of people who were to be our potential members. The last thing we needed was a book of rules and people voted into positions of false authority. The only authority we could have was respect, and respect in as much that if you fucked it up for us, there was a good chance you'd get a slap.

I'd like to tell you we had a master plan which fell into place, but truth is we winged it, learnt as we went along but progressed at such a rate nobody could have envisaged what was to come.

Many will know how the first meeting took place. I'd been toying with the idea of setting up a travel club from the 3 valleys, Rhondda, Aberdare and Merthyr, hence the R.A.M.S. plus the link with sheep shagging wasn't wasted on us. I honestly expected to start off with one bus to cover the three valleys and see how it went from there.

I phoned big Sam Murphy to ask him to get six boys from Merthyr, and also he asked six boys from the Rhondda, I was going to turn up with six of my mates and we'd meet up somewhere central and try and kick things off.

Well, we set a time and date and Merv Pearce arranged for us to use the cricket club in Pontypridd. Well the night came; I turned up in the car only to be met by Merv in a right sweat, "That twat Murphy has set us right up". "What's he done?" I replied, "Look over there" said Merv. And fuck me, rather than another dozen or so lads I was expecting, there were closer on 200.

"What the fuck are they doing here?" I said. I then found out that big Sam had been phoning every Tom, Dick and Harry (must have been reverse charge calls) He'd only told everyone that Sam Hamman was coming to meet everyone and give us a talk.

The Rise and Fall of the Cardiff City Valley Rams

When Big Sam Murphy finally turned up, he didn't bat an eyelid, no worries he said we'll think of something. "We!" What he meant was you'll think of something.

Merv Pearce hastily arranged with the club to open the upstairs function room, now that the planned corner in the lounge had got out grown by an extra few hundred guests, who were still turning up.

What was I supposed to say to this lot? 99% of them were expecting an audience with Sam Hamman, and they were now stuck with a speechless fat bloke from Aberdare.

I made up some excuse why Sam Hamman couldn't make it. I think I told them he was signing Ryan Giggs, so that kept them happy and stopped them smashing the place up. So, the RAMS were born. I told them about setting up a travel club that would be different from the typical "pop and crisps" image that other groups had been tagged with.

I told them I would arrange a meeting with Sam Hamman and that all those present would be the first invited. We took everybody's name and phone numbers and then hoped and prayed that Sam Hamman would come along.

Well, come along he did but with about two days notice, which to anyone that knew Sam was an improvement of two minutes notice and let's do it yesterday approach, that was his norm.

I arranged a venue; the Workingmen's club in Cwmaman. This was a newly rebuilt club supported by a lottery grant. It cost millions, had a purpose built cinema/theatre, a gymnasium, and three floors with various bars and function rooms.

The village of Cwmaman is well known for being the home town of the Stereophonics. Us Cwmaman boys would joke we had one pub, one club, one chip shop and one world famous group.

I had a mad panic getting people notified. But on the night, 300 plus people turned up and packed the main hall. Sam duly turned up and brought 2 club players with him, and also the football club chef Dennis and a van full of RAMS bollocks. Well anyone who was present will tell you that night was special. The atmosphere was electric and the place really was bouncing. Dennis had been sent to the club's kitchens to prepare Rams bollocks in pitta bread for 300 guests.

Sam had come into the club and we took him up the back stairs and onto the stage, the curtains were opened and the place erupted. It must have been 30 degrees in there and the condensation and perspiration was running down the windows. Even Sam was gob smacked and he'd seen more than most. He was bang in the heart of the South Wales Valleys, he'd had a few short notice trips and met a few dozen fans here and there, but this was massive.

When the singing and noise got just below eighty decibels, Sam grabbed the microphone, and spoke. The first words Sam spoke and the first time the vast majority of those present had seen him in the flesh was "what a great club, but the air conditioning is fucking shit". The whole night was mental. Sam was on his best form and the crowd loved it. After a good hour or so of the Vision as

Sam saw it, he then announced that he'd brought supper for everyone. He told them that they all had to eat a Rams bollock sarnie, and that anyone who refused, was to be seen as a traitor.

Oh fucking great, I'd been a vegetarian for 20 plus years and the first meat I was going to eat was a Rams bollock "Was it fuck!" If I was going to crack, it would be for a fillet steak or a much craved bacon sarnie, not a fucking Rams bollock. So I was a traitor to the cause before it had even kicked off. Great fucking start!

We called a meeting for the week Tuesday at the Thorne Hotel in Abercynon, a good central point for the three valleys. There was around eighty or so who came along. I had put an advert in the local paper telling people about this meeting and what we were aiming to do. I had a load of phone calls, but the one that stuck out was from a lad I new slightly. His name was Martin Jenkins or Jinx as he was known to us all. He lived in Aberdare and had played a good level of local football in between his regular sending's off and suspensions. He had stopped playing now and spent a lot of his leisure time training and running in half and full marathons, but where as his football playing days were over his love for watching Cardiff city had taken on a new level.

Jinx was like so many of us, hooked from an early age on Cardiff city, but looking for an extra adrenaline fix which Cardiff City rarely gave us during long, long periods. So playing sport was the solution as it was for so many others. Hence the regular 2,000 crowds during the Durbin and Ashurst periods.

Again like so many others amongst us, a good cup draw or a fruity home game against a team with a reputation for bringing some trouble with them and the crowd could quadruple in what seemed an instant. Local rugby and football teams must have wondered every now and then why they couldn't field a team. This is one of the knock on effects of having a successful team in the area. Nowadays, when 18,000 plus crowds are the norm, local teams from both codes must notice a difference. I emphasise both codes, because whilst most people out of the area think that South Wales is predominantly a rugby area, those of us that live here know that it's total rubbish. There are 4 times as many football teams as rugby teams around here, and even a lot of those lads playing rugby will tell you they prefer to watch football. Sadly a fair few of them will swear their undying love for Man U or Liverpool etc. but that's another debate.

Jinx was to become very much my right hand man, I make no apologies for saying I was the ideas and front of house man so to speak, but Jinx was the detail man, kept the records and finances on track and let me get on with my shit, we were a good team and had some great laughs together.

At that first meeting we started mapping out some sort of plan/structure on how to take bookings for away travel, because still at that stage that's all we were setting out to do. We asked for people to put themselves forward as Reps. Now we used the word "Reps" purely as a title for lads representing their mates, taking bookings, collecting the money etc. Little did these poor volunteers realise at the time but within months this would lead to an almost full time unpaid job.

The Rise and Fall of the Cardiff City Valley Rams

We split the Valleys up North and south so to speak, Mike "Stickey" Williams from Ferndale looked after one area of the Rhondda Valley, Peter "Mogs" Morgan took over the other area of the Rhondda Valley.

Mervyn "Merv" Pearce handled the Pontypridd area,

Russell "Mongol" Meeke was the Aberdare Rep and Keith Peacock the Abercynon Rep. Big Sam Murphy looked after lower Merthyr and Jackie Williams upper Merthyr.

Right, job done that was easy. First trip planned happened to be Peterborough away game. Not the most exciting venue and good four and half hours on a coach. Between us all we filled 3 coaches and we were up and running. Most people on each bus more or less all knew one another. They were from the same areas, but in some cases that could cause problems. The rivalry between villages and towns around here is legendary and to mix certain areas could have been risky. Things did happen at later stages, especially when we had to combine groups. For instance if there were 80 boys booked on from the Rhondda, then they may have to pick up 20 from another area to fill two coaches, but we got through those situations and learnt as we went on.

I had spoken to Simon Insole our F.I.O. (football intelligence officer) he was new to the job at Cardiff. He seemed sound and a good bloke but our side and their side (the Police) were walking a tightrope. There was always, an "us and them" mentality, not just with the Police, but also us and the club. In fact us and any sort of authority. If I had been seen totally buttering up to the Police, then any plans I had would have been dead in the water before we'd set sail.

I told Simon what we were doing for Peterborough and asked about the likelihood of the Peterborough Police finding us a pub where we could all turn up at and congregate. I made the offer of putting a £200 bond up for any landlord who was sceptical. That way, if there were any breakages or trouble, he could cover the costs accordingly. This was an approach I often used when trying to find pubs en route or at away venues. It worked a treat. No one took me up on the bond but I think that the offer itself showed that we were genuine.

This was also the approach I used to try and get coach firms to take us. Cardiff fans had a terrible reputation amongst coach firms, with buses being booked for shopping trips to places like Sheffield only for the driver to turn up and find 50 pissed up lads ready for a day on the rampage in Sheffield. He would be hoping to be home in front of the telly by 8pm and instead would find himself stuck outside a pub, club or police station at midnight under threat of his life if he didn't hang about.

It wasn't surprising that most coach firms were wary to say the least. The approach we took to overcome this was a similar offer a bond scheme and guarantee that any damage would be paid for etc. I managed to get a firm "Globe Coaches" from Aberdare to take us on board. One firm I rang from the Rhondda were horrified when I mentioned Cardiff City. The owner's reply was "he'd rather leave his coaches rusting in the yard than let them get booked for a Cardiff game" I can't understand where he was coming from; they'd only ever killed the two or three drivers as far as I'd known.

Risk element, what risk element?
QPR AWAY

The Ant Hill mob in full turnout. Total IQ 26

Mad Andies giving the big one at Wolves away

Sam with myself and Wayne on a walk up the Valleys

Big Sam, Macca, Vince and Robbie Bounds
keeping an eye on proceedings

Me, Big Sam, Ketty, Corky, and Terry Phillips
listening to Sam's Sermon on the beacons

Sam with Big Sam, Mogs and a couple of other
City fans after our Snowdon climb

Aberdare boys chilling

And they wonder why we call it the Ugly Bus

Big Sam and his Harem

Big Tom and Darryl

Dai Ton and Sicey, Rhondda old school

Corky, Dean, Gaffa and Dean

Gwyn and Corky

So Globe coaches it was then, and in all fairness they have been great with us and we still use their coaches even though it's done as our own groups again now rather than under the Valley Rams umbrella so to speak.

There were incidents occasionally, some were accidents some were just stupid vandalism, but we paid for any damage and built up the trust. Mind you every meeting we had, I would mention how much it had cost us and let the boys know it was their own money that was being wasted. This helped to make the lads more responsible and keep such incidents to a minimum.

Two bus incidents that spring to mind, and both involved Globe coaches and both involved "Stickey's" Rhondda bus. The Spurs trip away in the cup where we had 32 coaches was manic and I'll cover that in detail later.

Just as we were approaching the ground I had a call from Stickey, one of the boys on his bus had fallen down the stair well by the toilet on the bus and he'd split his head and the blood was pissing out. They managed to slow the bleeding, got him to the coach park in Tottenham and got him some first aid, job done or so I thought.

The next day I get a phone call off this lad, asking me for the number of Globe coaches. He told me that he wanted to report the accident and claim damages from the coach firm for his injuries.

Now it had turned out that this lad was steaming drunk and staggering up and down the bus aisle when he tripped and fell smashing his head. An accident as I'd see it, even if it was self inflicted, but his approach was that he wanted to sue the company for allowing him to drink and get drunk whilst on their coach because after all it was against the law to drink on a football coach.

I said "good on you mate, but where are you going to move to when you get your damages?" He asked why he needed to move and I told him that if he took that action then no coach would have anyone on board with even a wine gum in their pockets and he would be solely responsible for that. I told him he would be really popular and that I admired his courage in taking a stand to achieve justice against the driver who let him get pissed. I think the irony went over his head, but we heard no more of that one.

Another time after an away game I can't recollect, I had a phone call in work on the Monday morning from Globe Coaches. Wayne, the owner in all fairness was laughing when he told me the story. Apparently the driver had just dropped the last of the Rhondda boys off in Maerdy at the top end of the Valley; he was coming over the mountain and dropping down the other side back into Aberdare. Now these mountain roads are quite high and windy, a bit like the Swiss Alps without the snow and with a bit more litter and loads of sheep.

The driver was coming down the hill as fast as the road would allow and a dopey sheep walked straight out in front of the bus. He slammed on the breaks and he was aware of something flying towards him from behind. Well, he looked around and could see this wine bottle that someone must have left on the back seat flying towards him more or less four feet higher than the aisle. He moved his body to one side and the bottle flew passed him and took the windscreen straight out. He reckons he doesn't know who was most scared, him or the dopey sheep with a bus two inches from his face lying there with a bus windscreen on top of him.

Back to Peterborough and the first trip, Simon got back to me and said he'd spoken to Peterborough and they were well up for it and had found us a pub.

It was on the way to the ground and as each bus approached the police flagged them down and said get of here boys it will save you walking back from the stadium. Fuck me, what a start. I thought that some of the boys would come in their pants. Sensible coppers who were smiling and courteous and saving them a ten minute walk which would mean extra drinking time. The pub was great, they had a beer garden and everyone chilled out and mixed with one another. There were even Peterborough fans amongst us, something we take for granted now (mixing with other fans) but still a rarity in those days.

The game passed without incident (i.e. no deaths or fires). We got on the coaches and set for home. No police escort for 200 miles (and we've had a few of them). We were making our way out of the town when we saw one of our buses had stopped. The two other buses in our group stopped behind.

Was it a scrap? Had the bus broken down? No, far more important than either of those, they'd found an off licence. Well it was chaos! 3 bus loads one shop. You don't need me to paint the picture. It was buy one, pinch two free. Hopefully the chap covered his costs, but I don't think he made a profit.

This did give me a bit of a quandary. It was something that had gone on for years, but if we were to get any sort of regular travel set up, we would have to do something about it.

Now the drinking culture amongst our fans is well known, I make no excuses; it must be a Celtic thing. Welsh, Irish and Scottish it must be genetic. Drinking at football was seen especially during the Maggie Thatcher era as the root of all evil relating to football hooligans. This image was harnessed I think by the trouble especially in Europe and usually it seemed at most England away games. Everyone would congregate in the town square drinking inside and outside the bars, then several hours later, bang! Headline news and a major political issue. And yes whilst drink was a factor in the trouble, it doesn't have to go hand in glove that if you drink at football, then obviously you fight at football.

Laws were brought in which still exist. You could no longer drink on coaches whilst travelling to football matches. Great! So everyone who wants a drink, then goes by car, van, mini bus or train, still drinking, but now coming at you from everywhere. This meant that up and down the country, in most cases the fans that travelled by coaches were usually part of official supporters clubs and groups that would comply with these rules.

Did it stop them getting hassled? Did it hell! In lots of cases it lead to lazy policing, because the only info they had on who was travelling, was that supplied by the official supporters groups.

This often meant that police resources would be used to stop and search these coaches whilst all the "lads" would be having a ball doing their own thing here and there, happy days!

Now what we had all agreed amongst ourselves for the Peterborough game, was to make sure the buses were clean by the time they got to the ground.

This meant no drink to be hidden underneath (those days were yet to come).

The down side of this is that after these games had finished, the coaches would either be expected to stop at a pub for a good swig, or to find a supermarket or off licence for the boys to stock up for the return home.

Now this is exactly the scenario that we needed to try and avoid, so surely the easiest way around preventing these Ram raids (scuse the pun) was to allow the boys to have drink hidden underneath the coach ready for the home journey.

I couldn't see who we'd be upsetting. The bus driver would be happy, no stops with the possible impounding of his bus whilst the police looked at their CCTV from the supermarket that just got emptied. The boys on board were happy, more drinking time, less queuing and less fuss. The police were happy, they didn't have to escort us back to Cardiff or block every junction off, thus preventing us from leaving the Motorway in search of drink.

But it was breaking the law, Mad! These lads would be heading home on a bus doing 62 miles an hour, having a sing song and a drink with their mates, but that was breaking the law. Well change the fucking law then!

Everyone involved could see the sense in bending this law or at the least ignoring it.

We spoke to our police. They were responsive and could see the sense in it, but it did put them in an awkward position. They would be involved in pre-match meetings or correspondence with other forces and they would be asking them if they could break the law. So what police chief in which area would sign his name to any document giving us permission to break the law? The answer is none. They couldn't could they, but they could give a wink and a nod and many times they would see the sense in this method of getting us home and off their patch with as little risk as possible.

Now as we progressed at the Rams and grew in size, we were getting more and more input with the police and the club with regard to forthcoming matches. It got to the stage where we'd be invited to pre match planning meetings. Each one offered a different challenge. Some forces saw us as just a huge group of organised hooligans who were even more dangerous now that we had become such a huge group. Other forces could see the benefits of keeping us together and working with us.

We did offer a level of self policing; the older more well known lads could see the sense in preventing mindless hooligan type damage and pillaging. The message we put out was, if we were attacked, then we stuck together and never left a man down or took a backward step. All a bit of macho bonding, but the message we were trying to spread was, if there was serious trouble, we are in it together, but if you fuck about damaging or acting the prick, then you could fuck off, or even have a slap off one of us if you looked likely to mess up our privileges.

The extremes of this approach could lead to situations where if we saw one of ours getting mistreated by a bully boy copper, then he'd have a dozen bus loads of lads piling off the buses to sort it out. On the other hand if the coppers were fair to us and one of ours played up, then our own boys would sort it out and tell him to sort himself out.

It was a bit of a roller coaster. We'd go to a game one week where the police would stitch us up. You know the scenario; they'd say one thing and do another. Wigan away was a classic example, we took around 15 coaches there the first year, they found us a pub, and we stayed together. The pub was spot on, massive floor space and good grub; everyone was having a good time. The police came in the pub about half two, asked me to try and get everyone to leave en masse, which we did and walked to the ground in one large group, no problems and everyone was compliant.

When we were safely inside the ground I started getting phone calls off some of the coach drivers. The police had turned up in about six van loads.

They had opened up the storage areas under the coaches and were just chucking everything into one pile. Yes, there were loads of cans, loads of bottles, but also loads of personal belongings amongst the bags. In one case as we found out later one lad had put his insulin and syringe ready for his home bound jab to control his diabetes. This also had been stamped on and smashed before being chucked in the back of the vans for disposal.

Now there hadn't been a cross word and no problems anywhere before the game, yet suddenly when word spread of what was going on you then had 2,000 plus fans going mental inside the ground. The atmosphere had totally changed. I managed to find Simon Insole and he was tamping. He was in an awkward position, basically he's just a police constable, and up here in Wigan he had little if any power. He was only here to advise and observe. In lots of cases you would have the situation where the opposition police force would ask our police FIO's for information, yet when they gave this information or offered advice on how best to deal with our lads, the attitude often would be "who the fuck do these Welsh Police think they are coming up here and telling us how to police the game?" I have sat in on loads of such meetings and our police have always conducted themselves well. They may have been frustrated but it didn't show. They knew what worked with our lads and they knew what would cause problems. But they could only advise. The rest was up to the decision of the other force area. Never, ever did they try and tell the other force what they had to do, yet if you listened to some comments that came back to me from these meetings, you would have thought our police had gone in there taken over the meeting and laid down all these plans on how to deal with things. Total bollocks!

The whole thing of Football Police Intelligence, was basically a farce, sometimes nothing more than a paper exercise where the mind set was ingrained and all they wanted our FIO's to do was tell them how many were coming and at what time so they could lock up their daughters and hide the family jewels, point out the mad fuckers so they could arrest us before anything happened (it would have been easier at times pointing out the sane fuckers, less pointing to do then).

Anyway, back to Wigan, I managed to get outside the stadium, met Simon and we got over to the coaches where we met the Inspector who was glowing with self satisfaction at his wonderful piece of policing.

Simon couldn't say much, but no one could stop me. Instead of diving in raging I took the quietly smiling sarcastic approach. I said "you've done a good job there, I can see". He must have thought I was serious and replied that this would teach them a lesson (mind you they hadn't done anything wrong up to this point). He said this will show them they can't bring drink on the coaches to Wigan next year.

I said I totally agree and I would personally guarantee that none of our coaches would have drink on them next year. In fact I went on to say that the 800 or so Valley Rams we had brought up on masse would be back next year but not on coaches. They'd be in cars, vans, mini buses and trains. And he replied "Well even if that's the case we'll stop and search every car van and mini bus that comes into the car park and remove any drink.

"Great plan" I replied but do you believe for one second that they will come and park here? Because I know that next season they will now go into your city centre, park up all over the place, fill dozens of different pubs, meet up with all the lads off the train and no doubt have running battles with all your Wigan lads on route to the stadium. I also went on to ask what plans he'd made for after the game, and asked what I meant. Well I said "now that you've taken all the drink off these coaches, you have left these lads with the prospect of a four hour journey home on a Saturday night on a dry bus. So lots of these lads will now be searching for drink. That might mean when they get back they'll tell the driver to wait whilst they walk back into town. Or they get on board tell him to stop at the first supermarket or off licence or first pub they see with lights on, so I hope you have the resources to deal with it. Because you are going to have to block every route and exit from here back to wherever your jurisdiction ends and then let them drop on some other unsuspecting area". He was floundering now and I could see the reality of the situation coming home to him. It would be his head on the block if and when it all went tits up. He looked to Simon for some backing, and Simon just gave him a knowing look as if to say "he's telling it as it is".

He walked away a few yards and spoke into his radio, within minutes these six vans were back unloading these bags and cans etc. in one big pile on the edge of the car park.

The game ended and lots of our lot were after blood. They had heard about the looting as they called it and were no longer up for a bit of banter and compliance. In fact it kicked off on the bridge over to the car park and got right moody for a while. A police horse had knocked over an elderly chap who was walking back with his grand daughter and the lads were incensed. The blue touch paper had been lit and the banger was exploding. The next situation occurred when the lads saw the pile of shite that had been dumped in the car park. You now had hundreds of lads rummaging through this pile trying to find their bags or cans. And as for all this bollocks of looking after one another, when it comes to drink all bets are off. You had people who had lost four cans coming away with eight new ones, it was pandemonium!

Finally it got sorted and we made our way home, all apart from one bus load of us that had booked a night out in a hotel in Warrington, a place that was to become a regular stop off for us over the years and another story for later.

The following year when it came to playing Wigan away, their Police had already made contact with ours offering us the world. Someone had seen sense and had worked out the best way to deal with us. Some saw this as a sort of victory, but all most of us wanted was a good day out with as few problems as possible. It wasn't about one side winning and the other side losing. We should have all been on the same side. It was only a day out at the football.

I had to try and sell the police offer to our lot, some of whom were still up in arms after the previous year's treatment. These lads wanted to go up and show them how it could be if they wanted it that way. Luckily common sense prevailed and we had a great trip that year. But this sort of situation would arise more and more. We would get shafted by one area's force, so the next game in two weeks time in some totally different area they would want to extract revenge, even though that area had never given us a problem. It was a bit of a juggling act, but we didn't drop too many balls thank God.

We had some real strong characters amongst the membership, lads who would organise loads of their mates on a regular basis, but to formalise this organising was another thing. A lot of what we did initially was to harness the energy and effort these lads had been applying for years. The problem was very few of them wanted to be seen as authority/organisation figures. Titles and order was a new thing to most of them.

This is why we had to tread carefully. Words such as Treasurer, Chairman, and Secretary etc. were words and titles we avoided at all cost.

I became known as the spokesman. Jinx the money man and then the lads taking the bookings and looking after the coaches were known as the Reps.

It was a natural progression as we grew in size and numbers. Instead of loads of individuals making bookings you often had one lad booking on six or seven of his mates, so often each area Rep would have loads of sub-reps. It was working well and usually it would involve the Area Reps ringing me throughout the week firming up numbers as they went along.

It was working but it was chaotic. Part of our success and problem was the fact that we did not run the group as a business. If we had run it as a business we would have booked a set number of coaches, filled them as we went along, and if people had left it too late and there was no room on their local coach, then hard luck, they would have to travel elsewhere to get on another coach in a different area.

We tended to cater for everyone and if that meant we had to have 3 buses with 33 on each, rather than two buses with 50 on each, then so be it.

Where we were lucky was in the amount of coaches we were taking helped us to support this type of venture.

For example, if we had 15 coaches travelling, 5 may make a good profit and be rammed full, 5 may just cover the costs and the other 5 may be making a loss. Not the way to run a business, but our sole aim was to get as many fans as possible travelling, make it as easy as possible for them and as cheap as possible.

As we gained experience we learnt which area would have what numbers roughly. Also which areas would start the week with only a few numbers and then on the day before the game, ring up in a mad panic with an extra 40 lads looking for seats. I would say every time "look lads you were lucky this week to get a seat, but next game give us a bit of notice" did it work, did it fuck? And the next game would see the same lads doing the same thing.

Often I would be in work, and trying desperately to find another one or two coaches last minute to deal with the sudden surge in numbers.

One of the more annoying things though was the lads who would book on, then last minute find out the train was ten pence cheaper, book that but not tell the rep they had cancelled and he'd have a bus half full.

There often was no sense of loyalty shown by some and it was a case, as long as I'm okay then screw! you! In most cases I would describe these lads as the come and goers. Big games or big trouble would see them jump on board. Often they would be glad of the numbers to travel with, and not just the low cost and convenience we offered, but these lads were not the regulars and our regular fans would be back week in week out. This meant a great camaraderie was building up amongst each other. People were getting to know one another and it was great, but this did present us with new problems.

You would now get a group of lads from one area wanting to share a bus with another group from a different area. It was a bit "I want to sit next to Johnny type thing". And whilst it was great to see lots of groups building up this loyalty and trust in one another, again trying to arrange it all was at times mad.

On the down side of this, sometimes there was no way you could let two groups get on the same bus that just didn't mix. We learnt as we went on but often after one lad had been involved with a disagreement with a lad from another area etc. some of these groups had a hierarchy and power structure setup and meeting a group with similar structure was volatile, but again we got it sorted (usually).

Some people may be thinking now, I bet this is a Valleys v Cardiff thing, and they couldn't be further from the truth. We had more problems mixing lads from let's say the top end of one Valley, with the bottom end of another, and also one area of Cardiff with another neighbouring area. Saying that mind, whilst there may have been rivalry and some times bad blood between areas, when we were on our travels or at a game, if there was ever a challenge from rival fans or police for that matter, it was a case of hit one of us and answer to all of us.

Often a good tear up with fans from another club would help bring two of our warring areas closer together. There's nothing like helping each other out in a scrap to bring people closer together.

Another positive from this sort of set up, was the friendly competition that would come about. Reps and lads were taking pleasure in having the fullest bus or the biggest numbers. We encouraged this sort of competition and started giving areas nicknames and their own identity.

One such nickname started early on when I was at the Newport services on the M4 waiting for buses to arrive and group up for one of the games. Well the Rhondda bus pulled in and my God it was nuts! The only person on the bus that didn't have a scar and a broken nose was the driver and he had a crash helmet on. What a fucking ugly bus! That name the "ugly bus" has stuck ever since, and rather than be hurt by the tag, the Rhondda lads revel in it.

We had the AHM, the ant hill mob lads from Sengenydd, Abertridwr. The Suicide Squad from Abercynon (more about that name later) The Doh a Deer mob from Penarth, the Sunshine crew from Talbot Green, the Northern Alliance from the Heads of the Valley and the Breakfast Crew from Bryncethin. The Aberdare snakes, the Chaos bus, the Battle bus there were names and tags from all the areas. At its' peak we had more than 30 area Reps covering from Neath and Port Talbot down west, to Newport, Cwmbran, Magor and Chepstow in the East.

We also had a Rep for North Wales based in Anglesey. We even had the Australian branch of City Supporters affiliated to us. It was a great time and the identity and sense of belonging to a "different sort" of supporters group had captured the imagination.

We would arrange our meetings to fall just before the forthcoming away games, i.e. usually we'd meet on the Thursday or Wednesday before the Saturday away game, for mid week away games, we'd fit a meeting in as need be.

Now these meeting would be taken to a different area every time, this kept us in touch with all the areas and also gave people a chance to come along and have their say. It also created a fair bit of business for the pubs and clubs where we'd hold these meetings; it can't be a coincidence that 5 or 6 of our area reps were pub landlords. It made perfect sense for them to take on that role. People would be calling in during the week to book a seat etc. and often they'd stay for a pint especially as usually they'd meet a few other City fans there for a chat. Also the meetings when they came could mean up to 200 people turning up at times and all the revenue that would bring, and did I get a free pint? Did I fuck; I wish I'd been a bit more switched on at the time, lol.

In most places you would see a lot of the same hardcore faces, people would travel around from meeting to meeting, and these meeting were far more of a social gathering than a formal meeting so usually we would have a good laugh and a couple of pints to boot.

The Reps would be expected to attend because they would have the up to date bookings with them, mind you as I said earlier they would invariably change massively during the last day or two before the game, but it did help to have some idea how many were travelling. Also the Reps would then help to spread the word so to speak and anything we decided or talked about in the meetings could then be spread amongst the members when the were on board the next bus to the away game.

The network was spreading and working well, as the title of this chapter suggested "structure", what structure? For a group of our size to achieve what we did was amazing really and I don't think it could ever be re-created to that size or state again. It was the right time, the right place and a great time to be part of things.

The internet and mobile phone were essential to our planning. A lot of people may think that we still use carrier pigeons to communicate up here in Valley world, but the web site and message board we'd set up was having thousands of hits a week. The original web site had been set up by my mate and one of our founder members Dean Willis. He done such a good job on this site that it led to him being taken on and employed in the media department at Cardiff City. This meant we had to replace him due to a possible conflict of interest and to protect his position at the club.

A young lad Simon (Ely Valley Blue) Beddis took over the role as web master. He was a regular use of ours and the Mike Morris message boards. Someone who you would describe as a bit of an internet nerd, and a bit of a loner. But fair play to the lad he stuck at it and I think the experience and regular piss taking he took helped to bring him out of his shell. What things like this did show me, was that whilst a big majority of our members and regular travellers were from the rougher side of the road so to speak, other "normal's" would also enjoy being part of things and the whole set up gave different sorts of people a chance to mix, because at the end of the day, we were all Cardiff City fans. It also gave us some credibility at times when well spoken people who had good jobs could see how we would get treated at some games.

It was helpful when a lad may be getting some unfair treatment from a copper and someone would come on the scene and say "Excuse me Officer, I'm a solicitor, I have seen what has taken place and I would like to put myself forward as a witness". It often changed the way we would be treated. You could see the coppers thinking "Fuck me, they can talk English".

People outside of football may often have a set image of football fans or football hooligans as they'd imagine them to be if they were on one of our coaches, but they couldn't be further from the truth. Football is an escape, an outlet and a break from the "real world". This is why the prawn cocktail vision so many people in establishment hold, is so far from the vision that many true football fans want.

Having a couple of pints, letting your hair down, shouting and even swearing at a ref or opposing player whilst standing up in front of a plastic seat shouldn't see you classed as an hooligan. People don't seem to understand that we can have different hats for different situations. I have had a good professional job allied to the health service for many years, but on a Saturday I can let my hair down and become someone else for a few hours, that doesn't mean I'm any less good at my job, I'd like to think if anything it makes me better.

I have always felt easy mixing with all different types and classes of people, if you are happy with yourself why shouldn't you be. I think it's a blessing to be able to have a foot in both camps so to speak and whilst I'm more than happy to be seen as one of the lads, I wouldn't want to live like that 24/7. Equally so, I wouldn't want to live my "work, family type life" with no outlet for my energy.

This was one of the messages we were trying to get out to the world and also to our members. I am a big believer in the saying "if you tell someone often enough that they're bad, then they'll behave badly". Equally so, if you praise them and tell them they are good, they'll respond accordingly.

So it was a two pronged sword, keep telling Cardiff fans they are scum, hooligans etc. then if they behave like that, no one is surprised. In fact it's expected and so often this would lead to police forces up and down the country being put on full alert whenever we were due in town. The police would take the aggressive in your face approach to dealing with us. Our fans would react accordingly and return this aggression with even more aggression and it really was a vicious circle that no one could seem to break.

But Sam Hamman had shown me and a few others a different approach. It all sounds a bit corny and he would refer to us as his extended family and use the analogy of bringing up your own kids. He would say that if as a father you had six children and five were doing well and treading the right road, whilst one was behaving badly and taking the wrong road, you shouldn't exclude the odd one from your love. If anything you should give him even more love and attention and try and turn it around. However, you could only give someone so many chances and if they kept letting you down, then they would have to be ostracised from that family.

Now one of Sam's first moves when he'd come to the club was get Annis to book two buses for an away game at Mansfield, fill them with 100 of our most well known nutters and treat them to a champagne reception and prawn sarneys at a top a hotel in Mansfield before the game. Lots of people then and some still do criticise this approach, "Sam joins the Soul Crew" was one of the headlines. But I had gone along with Big Sam Murphy on one of these buses and could see Sam working his magic amongst these lads.

The message he was getting out was, it's our club, we need to all pull together, and we needed to have a new approach, wipe the slate clean and change our image.

He was giving everyone the chance to help change things and instead of the big stick approach and the "if anyone steps out of line approach" we will ban them for life and turn them over to the police approach that so many previous chairmen and owners had taken without success.

He even told the police that if they'd let him, he'd personally vouch for everyone who was currently on a ban. He'd put them in a section in the Grandstand and sit amongst them. Now the police and authorities were never going to have that, but Sam genuinely meant what he said.

The message we were trying to get out there was our future was in our own hands, and that it was us against the world, the Leeds situation and others helped to cement such matters and drew us all closer together. Therefore things like the Fans charter and the self policing aspect that we were using at the Rams started to pay dividends. We started stopping the childish type petty vandalism that had been a problem and the message we were spreading amongst each other was "we'll stick together, if any of us are attacked physically, verbally or even through the press, then we'd go at them as one" but to do this, we couldn't stand by and let others muck it up for us.

Every time a newspaper or TV and radio show made some accusation or painted a negative picture of us and the club, we'd be in their faces. One such occasion happened at the Western Mail and Echo offices, they had run a report stating that some trouble that had taken place in Bristol Town centre at 5.30pm on a Saturday afternoon had been caused by Cardiff fans calling in there on their way home from our game at Reading. No substance to this story, no great investigative journalism, just a rumour that they had heard and then printed as fact. Just another example, of give a dog a bad name, and doing their utmost, to keep our bad reputation in the public's eye.

Now the truth of the situation was, it would have been impossible for any City fans returning from Reading to have stopped off in Bristol, especially at that time. We were still in Reading Coach Park at that time and Bristol was at least an hour or so further down the Motorway. All the Coaches that had travelled to Reading that day had also been escorted (thanks to Thames Valley's finest football intelligence) in a convoy back to Cardiff. No coaches in this convoy had been allowed to stop anywhere on route until they got back to Cardiff, let alone call into Bristol for a set to. I'd already checked amongst all the lads who would have known if something had been planned or had actually taken place, and everything came back blank.

It came to light a few days later that what had happened was a group of lads from Mid Wales were up in Bristol for a stag weekend and they'd got involved in some scrape in a Bristol pub at the time in question. None of the lads involved were football fans, but they were Welsh so one and one makes ten in that case. So to an editor looking to sell papers, that fact then becomes a story that Cardiff hooligans had called in to Bristol looking for trouble yet again.

We contacted the editor of the newspaper and told him we were arranging for a protest to take place outside his office to discuss this rubbish article. In all fairness to him when we turned up to protest, he did come down in person and apologised. We told him how we felt about this and other such articles that were coming out on a regular basis, and he promised to take a fresh and fair view in the future. This wasn't the end of the battle, but it was a start and a small victory for us.

Another article that had been printed some weeks before and again got a few of us writing in complaining, was an article on the front page stating that a Cardiff City supporter had been jailed for 3 years for drug dealing in Ebbw Vale. Now you may think they could use such a headline especially if he was let's say selling these drugs at football matches or to his fellow football fans etc. But when you read the article it went along the lines of Mr A N Other aged 42 of Ebbw Vale was found guilty of etc. etc. It then went on to say that Mr A N Other who was unemployed had very few hobbies or interests but did mention that he used to watch Cardiff City when he was a teenager. You couldn't make it up could you, but they seemed to manage.

I became obsessed with answering or questioning any such reporting and I had plenty of support from Vince at the supporters club who was invaluable in matters such as this and dealing with the media. Mind you I always new that both of us were only one good riot away from being slaughtered by the media who were waiting if not praying for us to fuck up yet again. But luckily we started turning the corner and some of the steps we had taken to keep everyone travelling together and the police finding us pubs etc were beginning to pay dividends. Every chance we had we would highlight the positives. Little things like mentioning at this year's corresponding fixture with such and such a club. There were no arrests compared to the 4 the years before and there had been no reports of any trouble. I would also write to the match commanders at these games thanking him for his help and passing on my thanks to his officers that had policed the match so well. These commanders would always write back with a positive reply and we would use this to pass on to the media. Suddenly we were starting to look like angels and people actually did start looking at us differently, but not in all cases and definitely not in all places (don't mention the Wolverhampton or WMP words).

We were slowly turning the corner and we could start telling our members and supporters that their improved behaviour was being noted and paying dividends. We really played up on this, getting the message home to our lads that we must do all we could to keep things on this road and help prevent losing these benefits. We were doing our utmost now to big every one of our fans up. Telling them how each and every one of them had a part to play and if we were to get our new stadium, then they could all be proud of the help they'd given the club, or rather our club. We could no longer just blame others, or go around with a chip on our shoulders complaining how unfair things were. Yes, we did feel like second class citizens at times, but if the truth be told sometimes we had brought it on ourselves.

We were learning how the media worked and also how to work the media. Reporters have to report something, so let's feed them the positives and try and change the mindset of the masses so to speak. Sometimes when things did go a bit wrong and a situation may have occurred, I'd be waiting for a call on the Monday morning from the press asking me my opinions on what had happened etc. If the call never came and somehow it had slipped by the press unnoticed, it felt like we'd won the cup. It wasn't so much that we were scared of acknowledging some incident, my God little mishaps and mistakes would still take place at times. Rome wasn't built in a day, but when these events did get reported, it did set us back a little. It was a case of two steps forward and occasionally one step back, but we were moving forward.

I remember being told a story by someone involved at Cardiff City about a management type of course that he'd been on and it involved a word association exercise. Now it went along the lines that the lecturer would say a word and the class would have to link that to the first word that came into their heads and then write it down. The lecturer would say fruit, people would write down the answers, he would say car and so on, so on. Well when he came to the word hooligan, 99% of those present wrote down Cardiff City. The chap from Cardiff I think picked Millwall (as you'd expect lol) He said that he wanted to crawl under the seat and hide. But that was just how it works and when I refer to Millwall I justify that by saying "well they are known for hooliganism aren't they" as if that makes it O.K. to tar them with that brush, but not us. And that's just how it is, the slightest thing that Millwall fans do wrong is broadcast, exaggerated and helps to keep our mindset, it takes a major turn around to change people's outlook.

Well we had to at least try and change this image at Cardiff, and whilst we haven't totally won everyone over, at least a lot of people are now giving us the benefit of the doubt. A lot of us, me included love the image of our club and fans as being passionate, loud and even slightly intimidating. That doesn't mean we have to attack rival fans, smash up their buses etc. It doesn't mean we have to throw objects on the pitch. However, it shouldn't stop us screaming at every ref's decision, out shouting their fans, trying to get a rise out of their manager and putting their players off by glorifying in every miss kick or pass they make. To me and many others that's all a part of the game and helps you to feel part of the day's events, rather than stuck in some corporate box behind some sliding glass windows drinking fizzy over priced wine and eating finger sarnies. What's all that about?

Anything we can do to make their players and manager feel uncomfortable and give us a slight edge should be done, as long as it's legal.

I used the analogy of the Scotland fans to reassure myself that change could happen. Now during the 60's thru to the early 90's, Scottish football fans had a fearsome reputation, seeing them take over Wembley every other year for the home internationals. Digging up the pitch and pulling down the goal posts didn't help and also much like our lot in Cardiff, 90% of those present seemed to be totally pissed most of the time.

The maddest day I have ever had at the football took place in Anfield around 1975 when Wales were made to play their home game against Scotland in Liverpool because of trouble that had occurred at Ninian Park when Wales had played Yugoslavia. Some of the worse refereeing had seen a pitch invasion which resulted in a linesman getting speared by a corner flag, thrown incidentally by a lad who was now a member of the ValleyRams (I promise I won't give your name, Kev).

Now I knew things were going to be a bit different when travelling up the motorway to Liverpool to play what was meant to be our home game and for every Welsh coach on the road you would see two Scottish coaches. Fuck me, where were they coming from? I may not have an A level in Geography but I know Scotland is up north. So where were these thousands of Scottish fans coming from? By the time we got to Liverpool you would have thought they'd moved the match to Glasgow. There were tartan flags, bag pipes and kilts everywhere. We got there about 2pm ready for the 7.30pm kick off and already there seemed to be streets full of pissed up Scots everywhere. I couldn't begin to paint a true picture of what I was witnessing, but anyone who was there will know what I mean.

I believe the attendance that night was around the 60,000 and out of those, at least 40,000 must have been Scots with what must have been another 50,000 spread around Liverpool unable to get match tickets, and this was supposed to be our home game.

Well after our bus load had managed the walk to Anfield, or rather the military manoeuvre, because rather than a walk to the ground it was more like fight your way to the ground. You would get swarmed by loads of Scots either trying to buy your ticket, swap it for an empty bottle of iron brue or simply rob you of it.

As we got through the turnstiles into the Kop end which was supposedly given over to the Welsh fans, we had the obligatory search, but they must have been told to only search the Welsh fans, because once we got up into the kop, we became aware that at least half of it was full of Scottish fans who had at least ten bottles each and for some reason loads of sticks which I assume were flag poles. But fuck me, these flag poles all seemed to be six foot long and made out of two inch square timber.

Well once the first fight started, and it all had inevitability about it, there was chaos. I don't remember seeing a copper or steward in the kop just thousands of Welsh and Scottish fans who seemed to spend the whole match fighting each other.

One sight I'll never forget is after the game had finished (and we'd lost thank God, or I don't know if many of us would have got home otherwise) we got back to the bus and out of every five people on the bus, four had a bump or bruise. It was like a war zone. Every other person appeared to have a bandage or some sort of dressing on. Even the driver turned up with a bandage around his head and to make matters worse he was pissed. I kid you not two of the lads had to help him on the bus!

I had been around the block a little by this stage and had seen some of the maddest clubs such as, West Ham, Millwall, Chelsea and Leeds, but nothing had prepared me for Scotland's finest, a day I'll never forget.

But, something happened and I don't know what, but this image seemed to change overnight and suddenly the Scottish fans were now and still are seen as friendly passionate football fans, who are in the most happy, harmless drunks. Now whilst that may seem an idealistic view and those of us at first hand know that you can't take liberties with them. On the whole if they are treated properly, then the Scottish fans in general respond properly, but much like us, give them grief and then look out!

I was hoping in some way to replicate this change of image, I just wish they had produced a blue print of the methods that proved so successful for them.

Three years ago 2005 I had gone to a Football Supporters Federation meeting along with Corky to represent the Welsh branch in a meeting involving the four home countries. Lots of things were discussed such as a combined U.K.team in the Olympics (something we were all unanimously opposed to at the time) One of the other things we discussed was the fans embassies we run at away international games, something England had set up and years previously and had played a big part in helping reduce problems at England away games. We in the Welsh FSF had taken up a similar set up and it was helping, fans now had a central point to come to if they had problems and lost tickets, money or passports or even been arrested etc.

The Scottish Representatives said that they had looked at the possibility of setting up a similar venture but gave up when they realised they wouldn't be able to find any volunteers to stay sober long enough to man such an Embassy. Well all the rest of us cracked up laughing when they said this, but it was said in all seriousness and they couldn't understand what we found funny.

They do take their drinking serious in Scotland even our best drinkers came a poor second in comparison to them.

The next section was sent to me by a lad called Ben, a real character and very busy on the message boards.

Top of Form

When I supported the city I used to go with family friends as none of my mates or parents like the football. When I finally grew up and started drinking etc I never had any mates to go down the football with, they are all Liverpool or Man utd fans so finding someone who would go down the football with me week in week out was difficult and hadn't missed a home game up until this season since 1997 !! Then there were the RAMS, always went down the football home games on my own but as soon as you were on the grange you'd know everyone! Then I got into away games and travelling with the RAMS, best days of supporting the city and Wales away were these trips with the RAMS. I used to go alone, sit on a coach going from city road (Keith Harmen's coach) but after half hour you were the best of buddies with the people around you all having a beer etc. As trips went by Ii started to know more people and had kinda "football mates". Where ever we went I felt safe and everyone generally looked after each other! I started getting involved a bit more, being moderator of the RAMS board tops it off for me LOL LOL, but joking aside, walking up Snowdon raising cash for charities with all the lads, it was a great time. I felt apart of the big family of Cardiff city with Sam Hamman in charge and the RAMS, went to my first Wales away game in Dublin croke park and sharing a room with Gwyn, who I was told by a few he snored loud as fook, but I think after one night I got the title! lol Just things like that, none of that would have happened before the RAMS set up! You'd go away, herded off a train, got roughed up in the train station or even attacked by away fans!! and as a young lad in his teens that was scary But when the RAMS were up and running we all made great mates, you felt safe going away and by the end of the season you'd be good mates for life! yer we knew you weren't allowed to drink on the coaches, but we were sensible about it, got on the coach, had a few drinks. Before getting to the ground we got rid of everything and that seemed fine! well fine as in.... better that than all the lads going up in vans and trains, going to pubs, smashing them up and causing trouble putting city fans in the headline. This way of travel "the RAMS" meant we were all kept together, we could have a laugh and a beer together without hurting anyone, go watch the match and get back on the coach safely knowing that you've had a great day, you been able to have a drink (which all us lads like to do at the footie) and ain't been too much hassle! I really enjoyed those years going away and would do it again if the RAMS were back on track but since the last away game I went to without the RAMS on the train we had nothing but trouble from the police at stations etc and I can't be bothered with it all now to be honest! BEN.....

Chapter 5
The characters amongst us

One of the things we have never been short of around here is characters.

The Valleys area in particular has genetically formed the make up of so many people in this area.

If you speak to any of our lads who were former coal miners, the one thing they'll all say is that they miss the "craic". The work was dangerous and hard and the team work needed to survive was total commitment. However around this togetherness and team work was the non stop piss taking that was and still is such a part of life around here. It was no place for the faint hearted or delicate soul. If you couldn't take it and give it out, you either took to your bed or became a policeman (only joking Simon!)

It's always been the case as long as I can remember, we can knock lumps out of each other, we can tease and torment one another, but heaven forbid if an outsider is seen to do it. My God you only have to remember the miners strike, it was like open warfare, the police couldn't understand how they couldn't frighten and intimidate individuals on the picket lines, much like the fans at our football games, you push or hit one and you have to fight with all of them.

My God if your wife left you on the Friday for another man and you were on a bus to an away game the next day, forget sympathy, you would be the butt of the jokes all day. Don't get caught shagging a sheep around here because there's no hiding place (especially if you kept her to yourself).

A local story springs to mind from my village of Cwmaman. I used to teach a judo class in the village hall, and one of the kids was talking to me and he told me he was "Kathy Cotton reel's son". Well of course I was intrigued but thought better than to ask this ten year old where that name came from.

I found out later that when his mum had been a twelve year old girl, she had been having a bit of an exploratory fiddle with herself and a cotton reel (don't ask) and the cotton reel got stuck inside an intimate body part. She had to be taken to hospital to have the cotton reel removed and now thirty years on, not only is she still referred to as Kathy cotton reel, but her kids are known as Kathy Cotton reel's kids and they appear quite proud of it. The lady in question must be around seventy now and will never shake off this title.

Events like this make or break you, but either way events such as this inevitably lead to how your character develops.

The Rise and Fall of the Cardiff City Valley Rams

One of my best mates who died some nine years ago aged forty was a lad called Beefy. Lot's of City fans will remember Beefy, he was born with the brittle bone condition and this resulted in hundreds of fractures throughout his developing years. He grew to a height of only four foot eight, and having a best friend at six foot six, did attract a few looks to say the least.

He came from a family of seven kids and rather than be spoilt and pampered by his family, he was treated exactly the same as the others, he reckoned that his mother broke more of his bones than he ever did. She'd give him a wallop and if a bone broke in the process it was a case of "hard luck you'll behave next time".

He spent a lot of his time growing up in Penarth in a school for children with special needs. Well he was the school "daddy" running the protection rackets and fag taxing scams. Compared to lots of the kids there he was very fit and strong and definitely the maddest. He actually got expelled in his final year for streaking naked around the school swimming pool. I remember him telling me that when the school holidays would come around, all the kids would be excited to be going home because the majority of them lived in the school set up. He on the other hand would break his heart because he preferred life in school to his home.

Well he loved Cardiff City and whilst he was very mobile and could get around well, in later years due to all his previous fractures he did use a wheelchair more and more as his mobility became affected.

Well short of look on this as a problem, this wheelchair became our best friend. The list of places we got into thanks to that wheel chair is endless. We would turn up at an away game with fifteen or sixteen of us in a mini bus and find that all the pubs would be closed to away fans. Me and Beefy would turn up with the wheel chair and you could see the bouncer either thinking "fuck me they'll be no problem, he's got a wheelchair" or sometimes he'd be thinking "oh fuck if I don't let him in now, he'll play they are only turning me away cos I'm disabled card"

Well as soon as the first wheels would be over the door I'd shout "come on lads this nice man said we could come in" and fifteen lads would bundle in from around the corner, fucking priceless that wheelchair was.

We went out to Standard Leige for the cup game and had a ball. At one time we were outside the bars opposite the station where a lot of our fans had congregated. Around fifty yards or so further up this road was the bar the Standard Leige notorious Hells Siders (not) used to frequent. Now you didn't have to be Sherlock Holmes to work out that this is where it would kick off, and kick off it did soon enough.

It was a typical European type of fight you see at football whenever England are in Europe. Chairs, glasses and bottles flying back and for through the air, a bit of dancing around, and then a bit of steaming in with all guns blazing. Now up until the steaming in, the Hell Sider's were doing okay, you often see the European countries standing there trading missiles. But when it comes down to a full on scrap, they come a bit unstuck. Well anyway the scrap starts and the police come in from everywhere, job done or so I thought. However all they did was stop the fight, make everyone go back in the bars and then the police just drove off. They didn't leave even a token police presence outside and drove off as if now we've broken it up, it's all over. Well all it seemed to do was give our lads a chance to refill their glasses (after the bar owners had got replacement ones from the store room).

Bang! Ten minutes later it's all off again. It was mental this time. The police came back, but this time with water cannons, and it was funny as fuck seeing people being knocked off their feet and literally blown up the road by sheer water pressure. Fuck me the Rhondda boys were playing hell, they were soaked from head to toe and it wasn't even bath night.

Beefy and me were sitting outside drinking at a road side table and it was just like watching news at ten, but live from the studio so to speak. The police kept coming over to us asking if we were okay, and apologising for such scenes. After things had finally calmed down the police even flagged down a taxi for me and Beefy to get taken direct to the stadium. It was a great night, ringside seats and transport thrown in.

When we got to the stadium, they put us in the corner just behind a fence and directly behind the corner flag. There must have been another five wheelchairs in this section and a load of police who had taken up their positions there and they were just chilling and having a smoke in most cases.

Anyway about ten minutes into the match, this one lad gets brought in and placed in his wheelchair next to Beefy. Now this lad must have been in a terrible accident, he had no legs, both amputated above the knee, and one of his arms had been amputated at just around elbow level, but he was fucking huge, and not in a fat overweight sort of way but large muscular and well developed, which I found strange for someone with so many injuries.

He was wearing a Standard Leige shirt, and my God was he loud, he was shouting out at ten decibels above anything I'd ever heard and he was quite aggressive. Now I'd never seen Beefy scared of anything, but I could see this bloke was having an effect on him. I think it was a case of disabled section or not, this bloke was seen as a threat by Beefy, it was a bit of wheelchair hooligan equality.

Up until now this bloke had only spoken in French or Flemish or whatever else they speak over there, and actually it was shouting rather than spoken.

I said to Beefy "look, don't worry fella wheelchair or not, if he puts one hand on you (ironic because he only had one anyway) then disabled or not, I'll knock him straight out of that chair on his arse".

This made Beefy laugh and I think he felt a bit safer and braver now so he started shouting out his support for Cardiff whilst occasionally slagging off our Belgian friend, who Beefy assumed could not speak English.

Well anyway half time comes along and this bloke turns to Beefy and says in perfect English "I am the number one fan in Leige. Last season to thank me for my support, the team bought and presented me with a new Standard Leige kit" "oh, great" said Beefy, "a full kit?" he enquired, "yes" said our friend, and quick as a flash Beefy asked "do you want to sell the socks?"

The Rise and Fall of the Cardiff City Valley Rams

Well I thought two of the coppers were going to swallow their fags, everyone in ear shot were trying hard not to laugh out loud. Beefy just sat back in his chair, lit himself a fag and smiled, one up to the number one Spaz, as he said to me later.

One trip I remember where the wheelchair provided us with some entertainment was Stockport away. It was mid 90's and I think it was the first game of the season. It was a boiling hot day and not the best time to be stuck on a motorway in a transit van as we were that day.

We had been making good time until we hit the M5 and M6 merging directly by Walsall's stadium.

This spot is a notorious place for hold ups and today was the mother of all hold ups. I don't think we had moved a mile for over an hour. We had 15 of us in the van, 13 in the back and me and Beefy in the front. We had the side doors open to let in some air and suddenly one of the lads Jeff Hill, shouted "watch this now". He gets the wheelchair out, sits in it and starts propelling himself up the motorway past all the gridlocked cars. Now, most of these cars had their windows open and you could see the drivers shaking their heads with amazement at the sight of this wheelchair being driven up between the rows of cars and overtaking them.

He'd gone about 50 yards when he stopped next to a chap who was looking out of his window, Jeff acknowledged him and said "fucking traffic, I was making good time till here" and off he goes again. Well we were creased and for the next few days I was half expecting to see a clip of this on TV, that was one that obviously the overhead cameras missed.

Another memory from traffic hold ups, concerns an away game at Scarborough. Now, that's a hard slog on a good day, let alone after being held up. Some people can't see the attraction in travelling around the country in such ways, but those of us that have done it will remember the craic we'd have during the trip almost as much as the game. Basically it was just like being in the pub, but in a pub that was doing 70 miles an hour (I nearly wrote 80 mph then, but I thought I may get in trouble, lol).

We must have still been 30 miles or so from Scarborough on a dual carriageway, we had slowed down to a stop start crawl and the boys asked me to pull over on the side for a piss. I told them they'd have to wait, just to wind them up, but gave in when two of them opened the side door and started pissing out as I drove.

Most of them jumped out and were doing their stuff when the traffic started to crawl off again. I thought I'd pay them back and started driving off. Well, a few panicked and start running behind still pissing. A few knew I'd wait and just laughed. Anyway the van filled back up and I started driving as the traffic had sped up slightly, when someone shouted, "Jeff Hill's not here". I thought "the little twat, he's done a double whammy on me now" he knew I wouldn't leave him, so I pulled over and waited to see if he'd appear running along the road around the bend that we now found ourselves on.

One minute, two minutes, time was passing and I was getting the hump now, when suddenly one of the boys screamed out "there he is". I looked up the road but couldn't see anything, and Russell said "not that side try the fast lane".

I looked across just in time to see Jeff sitting on a jet ski that was being towed on a trailer up the fast lane. The bloke driving was oblivious to this and didn't realise what was happening until he had to slow down and Jeff cool as fuck just jumped off and waited for us to catch up. This was the trip when it was either Scarborough's first or second year back in the league. The one thing I do remember about their first game in the league was seeing a Wolves fan up on the roof and then falling through it down on to the terracing below. I can't remember if he died but it was shown on every TV channel for ages afterwards.

Now, when we got to Scarborough that day we swamped the place. It was a new ground for most of us and our away numbers always increased accordingly. We got into the ground quite early and some of our boys had brought in a football from the van and they were having a kick around in between the side and the end stand. Everything was relaxed when I heard a tannoy announcement "stand still. Would the gentleman on the roof please stand still" I looked up to see one of our lads Gary Meeke (or Flicker as we called him, because he was a quiet lad until he'd had 3 pints, then it was as if someone had flicked a switch on, because he used to turn fucking mental). Now he'd gone up there without a second thought to get the ball back cos he'd kicked it up there by accident. Well it was pandemonium on the ground around us. We had every steward, loads of coppers and even two firemen. We only needed the coast guard to have a full set. Flicker couldn't understand the fuss. He must have been the only person in the world that hadn't seen the Wolves fan fall through that very same roof not long before.

They finally got him down, and they were so relieved not to have some more headline news, they just let him and the lads carry on with their kick around. Mad days!

We had some right headers in our ranks and I'm sure some of them had death wishes. One of our earliest games as the Rams was QPR away on a Tuesday night. We planned to stop off in Acton for a pre match piss up and go in from there by tube and then meet up after the game with the buses that would drive to the stadium whilst the game was on. That way we'd have more drinking time and less time stuck in traffic. Mind you, the amount they would drink on the bus there didn't seem much point, but they do love a good wander.

Now these were the very first few weeks of our getting together and we were still learning about each other and getting to know who was who etc. We only had around five buses there that night, a nice manageable amount. There was a big green central area in Acton where we congregated and found a pub. It was a good spot because you could see the other buses approach and guide them in. Well, in the distance I could see what looked like one of our coaches coming around the corner. This was confirmed when I became aware of someone standing on the roof of the bus surfing.

I thought the driver will be well pissed off when he pulled in. I waited for the bus to pull in and clocked it was the Ferndale bus which Stickey was running as the Rep. I waited by the door for Stickey to come out and next thing it was him climbing down off the roof. Fair play you can't say he wasn't leading by example. The driver was cool about the whole episode and all he could see was the huge tip he'd get for having a laugh instead of being a twat (or doing his job properly lol)

Stickey's example didn't end there mind. After the game we had all got on the buses and the coppers were trying to get us out of there, when one of the Ferndale boys come running up to me saying "we can't leave, Stickey's not here". I thought he may be sorting out some trouble or getting some stragglers sorted, so I spoke to the main copper and said "could you do us a favour, the chap who is running the bus and stewarding it for me is running 2 minutes late but he'll be here shortly, can we just hold on for him?" The copper wasn't best pleased but gave us a bit of grace. I told the copper that this lad was sensible and must be held up on some issue or other, and then the next thing I notice is Stickey bouncing up the road off the wall in a total stupor. I went and got him and I could see this copper looking at me and shaking his head in disbelief.

We found out later that Stickey hadn't even got to the game. He'd woken up pissed in some back street alley in West London with £700 of bus money wedged in his pockets and with a few winos for company. He didn't know where he was or what he was there for. He staggered to a phone, phoned his missus up back in Ferndale and she had to tell him where he was and what he was supposed to be doing. It all worked out well and surviving things like this helped us to forge an identity. I don't think for a minute we could have carried on at that rate, but it was just like going abroad on your holidays for two weeks. The first night's always mental and then you settle down to just normal over excess.

QPR must bring out something in our lads because on the way home the Aberdare bus was heading back down the M4 making good time when Mart the Dart made his way down the front and said to the driver "do us a favour mate can you pull over on to the hard shoulder but do it really slowly because one of the lads is on the roof". It had turned out that Brian from Abercynon had climbed up through the rear sunroof and was crawling up the roof of the bus hoping to get back in through the sun roof at the front of the bus. Well they managed to get him back on board safely and the driver continued his journey, one eye on the road, the other in the rear view mirror checking on sun roof escapees.

We made an example of Brian and banned him from the next away game. It was a coincidence that he was on holidays at the time and couldn't have attended anyway, but that's beside the point. Brian was an ex Para and he'd done a few tours of duty in Northern Ireland. (I think he'd done one too many in my eyes, because he was nuts) Often we'd turn up at 7am to pick him up for an away game and he'd be pissed getting on the bus. He would sing football songs from start to finish and must have had the best repertoire I've ever heard. He knew them all and then some more. It was after his roof climbing exploits that the Abercynon suicide squad got their name. Luckily most of them try far safer methods of suicide and simply tried to drink themselves to death.

Another incident linked to QPR involved a chap called Mel. Mel lived in the Hengoed area, he was mid forties and a great bloke, loved a pint and had a good job and was very much a part of what we were doing. One match at QPR, I was walking up to the ground along with Corky and a few other lads when we could hear someone screaming in pain from the back of a police van. We tried finding out what was happening but couldn't get any sense of the coppers around the area. When we got in the ground we found out that the bloke in the van was Mel, he had been arrested on entry for being drunk but what he was trying to tell the coppers was that his twelve year old son had just gone in through the turnstiles and had walked on oblivious to the facts his dad had been refused entry. The more he tried to explain the more he wound the coppers up, resulting in his arrest, but during the arrest the coppers pulled his arms behind his back to cuff him and snapped his humerus bone in the process. They wouldn't listen to his screams of pain and simply took him the police station, any way we got his son sorted, got someone to stay up with Mel, who on being seen by the desk sergeant was taken straight to hospital for urgent treatment.

This whole case ended up with Mel getting several thousand pounds in damages. Now several months later Mel had recovered and the plaster and sling had been removed, he was ready for his first away game back with the lads, unfortunately for him the first game back was West Ham away.

The match as expected was a bit tense and one of the many events of the day was the mass punch up under the stand at half time, I wont labour the background to this scrap but it involved a good fifty or so of the Mets finest heavily armed Robbo cops and some four hundred of our no necks having a full on toe to toe scrap. Now the majority of our fans still in the stand were oblivious to these events, and unfortunately for Mel he was one of them, he was making his way down the steps to the concourse and as he put his head around the corner he got whacked by a coppers staff, blood everywhere and Mel sparked out on the floor. The poor bastard was carried out on a stretcher, we didn't know whether to laugh or cry.

One of our reps Darryl from the Rhymney area in the Valleys was a real beauty. He lived on a council estate in a real rough area. I remember him showing me the first time I went there, a house across the road, and he said "See that house. That bloke's the only one on the estate that's got a job". He reckoned on his first day in work all the rest of the people on the estate got up early to clap him to work. It would have put that show Shameless to shame.

The flat Darryl had, was like fort Knox. It was camera'd up, alarmed and short of a moat and trip wires, quite a little fortress. Mind you, it didn't stop the police from having the door in once a month. He used to pop down the station some mornings to get some tea bags back if he had visitors. He bordered on paranoia with his security, but quite often his hunches weren't far out. However some of the better ones which had us chuckling was the disabled copper in Asdas up in Wigan. Now Darryl would run the bus for us week in week out, but most of the time he wouldn't go inside the stadium. In fact I don't believe he even liked football that much. Now in Wigan whilst we were all inside the stadium watching the game, Darryl along with his girlfriend at the time (that was before she had him jailed) went shopping to Asda. Well shopping in this case, was six trays of grog for the trip home.

Now as they went in Asda they passed a bloke in a wheelchair. Darryl turned to his girlfriend and said to her "see that bloke in the wheelchair; he's an under cover copper". "How do you work that out" she replied. "Look at the soles of his shoes" he said. "They have got wear on them. How did he wear them out if he's in a wheelchair". Fucking spot on, detective Darryl.

Another time when we were playing Norwich away, a couple of buses stayed up in Great Yarmouth for the night in a hotel. Everyone except Darryl went out on the lash. Darryl stayed on guard looking out of his hotel bedroom window. When the lads started getting back in the early hours, Darryl told them that he'd spotted a man walking passed the hotel on the opposite side of the road with a dog and he was convinced this bloke was the desk sergeant from Blackwood police station and that he'd been sent up there to keep an eye on them, Yorkshire terrier and all. The other story that springs to mind was the last minute friendly the club arranged away at Hibs. It was done within days after some other team we were due to play pulled out. Now we put a quick bus together along with some of Vince's regulars and lots of others of us went up in cars and on the train to make a weekend of it. Well when we got to a pub near the ground which was a bit tasty to say the least, Darryl was bang on form. He turned to Corky and said "see that bloke over there" and Corky said "that one with the two young lads in Hibs kit" "aye that's the one" he said, "football intelligence from Cardiff". Corky said "don't be so daft mun, his kids have even got Hibs kit on". "All paid for out of expenses to throw us off the scent" said Darryl.

Big Sam one of our most well known faces and a real help (depending on how you describe help, lol). Now whilst a lot of us consider ourselves as out and out Cardiff fans, Sam is totally one eyed and blinkered, always believes that things will turn out Ok, always trusts people are genuine when it comes to Cardiff matters, until proven different then look out, he's stormed that boardroom more often than the Mexicans did at the Alamo. Even if we are three down he's convinced we can pull it back. Mind you if we are one up with ten minutes to go, you won't see him in the ground but more likely pacing up and down in the toilets like an expectant father. You daren't say a negative word about the City in Sam's earshot, otherwise you are called a traitor and heaven help you if he thinks you watch an occasional rugby game on the telly. A lot of us dislike the rugby set up in Wales and not so much the game as the media and political hype that goes with it, but Sam sees rugby as the devil incarnate. Now one of Sam's strength's is his the famous lists and numbers he keeps.

You would never catch this bloke for a penny when it comes to money. After we had been running a few weeks we realised that we needed some details of people who were travelling with us, now we weren't in it to make money but we did need a little in the kitty to bail us out and keep things running, it would also help us to get match tickets and the like for these lads, also if we needed to ring them or e mail etc, it would need some details to help us get in touch. I think we were only charging 2 quid for the first year's membership the price of a pint of beer in those days.

Now what we agreed on was that whilst the buses were on route to an away match, it would be the ideal time to go around these lads whilst you were collecting their bus fare and ask them to write their details on a sheet of A4 paper, Fuck me a name, phone number and address or heaven forbid an e mail address anything would have helped.

Well the next meeting came along and all the Reps handed their lists in, Jinx had collected Sam's list and burst out laughing. Now we weren't expecting audited accounts or Shakespearian prose, but Sam's list was a classic.

It read something like, Jonny from Aberfan, Stevey from Treharris etc. then half way down the page you had something like Jonny's mate and Jonny's brother, fucking priceless.

Stickey from Ferndale on the other hand had presented his list in copper plate English with all the details filled in, the only problem was out of the ninety members or so he was looking after, forty five of them were serving club or Police bans

Now Sams memory for all things cash is amazing, but numbers on buses and who's coming etc is another thing. We have all learnt that if Sam tells you he's got 30 booked for his bus, it could wind up anywhere from ten to eighty. His famous last words are "don't panic, it will all be ok". Some games I'd be fifty miles into the trip when the phone would go "Gwyn, we are still in Cardiff, we got sixty on the bus and there's another twelve to pick up in Cardiff east services".

Many's the time I'd have to speak to the driver on Sams bus, offer him a bribe to make it worth him losing his licence, then get these lads up to a service station or somewhere I could hold up some of the buses to take this over spill. Mind you I nearly set the record for over crowding myself by accident when I'd booked a 75 seater double decker for the Aberdare load to Barnsley and we had 114 on there until we could off load some in Monmouth. But when things like this happened, whilst stressful at the time, we always seemed to get out of it.

When we had got up and running, we needed to have some sort of order for membership. Now, again I repeat myself, the last thing we could be seen doing was to get too formalised too established and have too many rules and regulations. Part of the image was being that bit different from other organisations. But we had got to such a size that we needed a little bit of organisation. The club was really supportive at these early times and a lot of that in fairness, was due to Sam Hamman. He was totally supportive in what we were doing and had told everyone at the club to help us in anyway they could. However we couldn't abuse that help and been seen to take the piss.

Now some of our lads would take the piss at every chance they could. Part of the structure the club had to impose after the Leeds fiasco was to issue membership cards. Now if you weren't a season ticket or a card carrying member, then you couldn't get an away match ticket. However people will find loop holes in any system and the way around this was to get a member to buy a ticket in their name and let you have it if they weren't going.

Now at the Rams we were putting together a nice little data base of our members' names and numbers etc. That way we could tell who was and who wasn't going and we could occasionally use this to our benefit to get some tickets and help lads out occasionally.

Now this was meant to be used for lads who live away, such as the Hollyhead lads and other spread around the country who sometimes may only be able to take in one or two away games close to where they lived.

Now we didn't mind doing that now and then, but even some of these started taking the piss. I would get them tickets and arrange to meet them outside a ground somewhere and they would stagger up pissed about ten minutes into game with me stuck outside waiting like a knob, whilst they rolled out the same excuses as last week for being late. The other side to that coin was when I would be taking tickets to an away game and find out the lads who'd ordered them had gone in the ground because they'd opened a pay on the day turnstile. So I'd be stuck with half a dozen match tickets. Also some lads would ring up the night before the game saying they'd swopped shifts or their wife had died, so they could come to the game now and could I get them tickets now that the ticket office was shut.

Well, part of our aim was to get as many city fans to these games as possible. So, usually we would sort something out. Then what would happen would be the same lads ringing up every week doing the same thing. It makes me think how many wives can you have that die that often. It got so bad that it got to the stage where they wouldn't even phone up the night before. They would just turn up at the away ground and ask me for a ticket. When I would ask had they booked it, they'd say they had been too busy. They'd be gob smacked when I told them I'd got none left and it was my fault then for letting them down. I was too trusting and too helpful if truth be told and people were taking advantage. Others close to me could see what was happening but I believed and trusted people's integrity more than I should have.

Things did change a few years later and when Corky came on board as Secretary and took on a lot of this type of thing for me, he really got to grips with that side of things and people had to wipe their own arses so to speak.

Another QPR story springs to mind and even though it's out of context, I'll tell it now. I think it was in our second or third year under the Rams umbrella. We had taken around 15 coaches up on yet another night match. (they always seemed to be night matches in those days, possibly because they thought less of us would travel. But we would take the same numbers and people would see it as an opportunity to drink more because it was a later kick off. So now they've worked it out and the last few years have been back to a Saturday kick off). The pre match planning had worked well. We'd arranged for the buses to drop us all off outside the Walkabout pub in Shepherds bush. Straight off the bus, straight into the pub, and an escorted walk on masse to the ground about 7pm. Job done and it did look impressive to see close on a thousand of us being walked up the high street happy as sand boys.

Whilst the game was taking place the police had brought the buses up to one of the roads near the stadium and after the game we were escorted back to our buses. Unfortunately, the Met in their wisdom hadn't worked out that most if not all of us, wanted to get back on the same bus that we'd come up on. It does make it easier when all your stuff is on that bus and the bus also drops you off near your home.

The Met's vision was at the time, just get the first bus full and get it out of here and then fill the next one up, no discussion, no planning and chaos ensues. They couldn't understand why the boys were having none of it and they caused a full scale tear up from nothing.

Now during this tear up there was the usual split heads and dog bites, sirens all over the place, hundreds of locals hanging out of the apartment block windows watching all the action. Suddenly out of the corner of my eye I could see one lad take a right whack off a coppers staff, down he went head split open and bleeding. A couple of us ran over to help him and so did another copper who had seen what had happened and I think he too was genuinely concerned. "Are you okay mate" the copper said to the lad. "Fuck off you twat" came the reply. "It was one of yours that did this to me". Well the copper was a bit narked with the reply, but the lad was getting even more narked. In all fairness, I think the copper was trying to help but this lad was having none of it and getting more and more wound up. Eventually the copper had enough called for help to now arrest this lad who he'd intended helping.

A van came screeching up to a halt, they cuffed the lad on the floor and then tried to pick him up, but he was screaming his head off. We were trying to get help him but there was a ring of coppers around him having none of it.

Anyway we established why he was screaming. When the van had screeched to a halt, it had only left a wheel over this lad's foot. They were trying to pick him up and his foot was stuck under a van. We didn't know whether to laugh or cry. But the best was yet to come. This lad got charged for his trouble and had to go to court. I didn't know this lad and he hadn't made contact about helping him with his case as most did, but we did have some other lads who'd been arrested that night and they returned from court with a great story.

It had turned out, that this lad was a South African, he lived near Loftus Road and that night he was just returning from the shop with his ruck sack on his back containing eggs milk and the like. He could see all the buses ahead of him parked in the road but had to pass through them to get home. As he was walking passed, one of the coppers had grabbed him and tried to put him on a bus. Now, he had tried to explain to this officer that he hadn't come on a bus and lived just down the road. But the copper was having none of it. Now those of us that have been there will be nodding and thinking I've been there and done that. Others will be thinking that's ridiculous, things like that don't happen, but when you get caught up in situations like this, having an explanation or even a valid argument isn't an option. You either have to fight your corner or hide and leave your mates fight theirs. Discussion and common sense aren't part of the equation.

Now this lad had wound up in court and had his chance to explain and put his case forward and see how British justice worked. What actually happened was he received a one hundred pound fine and a three year ban from attending any football matches in England and Wales. Not bad for someone who had never attended a football game in his life.

Now Corky's name has popped up a few times, so it's only fair to give some low down on him. Corky has always been one of the lads, but one with a fair mind and the last person you'd describe as a hooligan, but like so many of us that turn up week in week out, he would automatically be seen by some coppers at away games as a likely candidate.

Now one thing that may have helped Corky to stay out of trouble is the fact that at the age of 20 or so, he had to have one of his legs amputated below the knee after an accident whilst working underground in a local colliery.

Now the whole story of losing the leg, whilst being tragic, is also ironic as well. The day the accident occurred, Corky wasn't meant to even be in work, but he had managed to swap a shift so that he could catch an away game later that week. Mind you it didn't hold him back too much and he still managed to get over that 8 foot wall at the back of the old Den in Millwall a few years later, when him and four others were faced with jump over the wall or face the hundred nutters with more knives than Kitchen's Direct who were heading towards them.

Now artificial leg it may have been, but it wasn't fucking bionic as he found out when he realised that the wall, whilst eight foot high one side, was thirty foot high the other side. Luckily the fall was slowed down by a load of trees. He reckons he would have had fewer injuries if he'd taken a good kicking off the friendly Millwall chaps. He said that he had so many twigs and leaves stuck to him, the camouflage helped him blend in and escape. He reckons he was in so much pain that even the false leg was aching.

I remember one occasion walking with Corky and a few of the lads along with Sam Hamman up along the rivers edge in the Brecon Beacons one Sunday morning. Suddenly, we heard a yelp and a splash, only to see Corky face down in the water's edge with his artificial leg sticking up in the air and the foot piece stuck firmly between two rocks. Harry Hill would have had a field day with that one if we'd had a video camera.

One of Corky's opening lines used to be "what's got three legs and likes chips?" "Me and my girlfriend" he would answer.

He told me once about one of his girlfriends who actually believed him when he said that he had an artificial leg but a real foot. It took her a month to work it out.

A great Corky story which must be told involved a trip up to Walsall with his young son and one of Corky's mates in the car. Now, Corky had been driving up the M50 in his fifty pound bottom of the range Ford Cortina.

The car started over heating due to a fan belt slipping. Corky phoned the RAC and told them that he had broken down and asked for some help. They told him they'd try and get someone there within the hour.

Corky was well pissed off now as he thought he'd miss the match kick off. He asked could they get there any quicker and the operator said they could only do that if it was an emergency. He asked what constituted an emergency and the operator replied that if the car was in a dangerous position, or smoking and likely to catch fire then they would have to get there at speed.

Well as far as Corky was concerned, this was an emergency, so he replied that the car was smoking and that he thought it was likely to catch fire, "Okay" said the operator with some urgency in her voice, "we'll get some one straight out to you". "Job done" said Corky smugly to himself as he

Walked the half mile or so back to the car from the emergency road side phone. Just as he got within yards of his car he could see in the distance three fire engines with lights and sirens blaring and heading towards him. "Oh fuck!" He had to think on his feet now (or in his case, his foot) and the solution he came up with was to open the boot of his car and try to set fire to an old cardigan in the boot using a cigarette lighter. Well luckily for him that didn't work and he was surrounded by firemen looking for the flames whilst being amazed that he'd left his son sucking a lollipop in the back seat, whilst his mate was sat in the front reading the Daily Mirror.

They gave Corky the benefit of the doubt and told him possibly something had got wrapped around the exhaust and might have caught fire, but fallen off back up the road. Whilst all this was going on, the firemen had shut the M50 for safety reasons and the traffic was backed up for miles.

He made the kick off, but he reckons it was a close run thing, because he'd got caught up in all the traffic that had been held up behind them on the motorway and he even blamed the firemen for over reacting and shutting the road.

Now most of us that know Corky well, will know that he will have enough stories and quotes to fill a book on its own. But, another day possibly. However, there are two more tales,I must write before its back to business.

Corky, whilst mad as a box of frogs, is one of the most loyal friends you could have. He's seen me through a few divorces and it got to the stage after the last one, where I even moved in there for a couple of years to get my head together.

Now that period was a great laugh and the house more or less turned into the Rams HQ. There were people back and forth at all hours and Sam Hamman spent as much time there as he did down the club. I swear he bought half the Cardiff team using Corky's phone.

Corky however loves his soaps, almost as much as he loves his football. Coronation Street, Eastenders, Emmerdale, and the Bill. So the hours between 7 and 9pm were off limits. He'd hide out in his back kitchen come dining room and office eating his dinner, watching the soaps and typing away on the various football message boards.

Well this one night in question, I got home from some function or other at around 10.30 pm, opened the front door with my key, trying to make enough noise to give him some warning (the old 30 second adult channel alarm period, just enough time to pull your zip up) and I couldn't fail to see on the stairs facing me, a tray which had a load of chips and a battered fish with one bite taken out of it.

I shouted up the passage, "Oi Cork, what's the story with the fish and chips?" Well when he told me I doubled up. What had happened was he'd timed his night like a military operation. Up to the chippies at 6.45pm, back in time to settle down for supper and Emmerdale farm at 7pm. Problem was at 7.02 pm, someone starts ringing the door bell. But Corky's got a plan. He decides to answer the front door with his supper on the tray held firmly in his hands, that way he can get rid of any unwanted visitors and show them he's in the middle of his meal.

Luckily, or not in this case it was just a delivery of sorts, no delay just sign the form and back to the telly. Well he puts the tray down on the stairs signs the form and returns to the kitchen. Hold on a minute he thinks to himself as he sits back down, where's my fish and chips? He reckons he spent the 20 minutes looking for his supper, before giving up and making himself a pot noodle. Mad as a March hare.

The last story (and he'll hate me for it, but fuck him, lol) loads of us had gone out to Dublin for the Wales Ireland game, the first football match ever to be played at Croke Park. We were there for 4 nights but by the last night Corky had cracked and whilst most of us headed for the Temple bar, Corky took to his bed for an early night (or so he reckoned).

When it came to check out of the up market hotel the following morning, Corky went up to reception to hand his key in and leave, but as he turned to walk away, the rather snotty male receptionist said "excuse me sir, there's a bill for 20 Euros outstanding on your account". Corky's up on his high horse now, but unfortunately all this is taking place in front of Chris Catterson the Rep for the Sengenydd Ant Hill Mob.

"I haven't ordered anything" said Corky, "if someone has charged a drink to my room there's no way I'm going to pay for it.

"No sir" replied the snotty receptionist, "it wasn't for drinks, it was for last nights viewing of the adult channel in your room." Corky replied "I didn't watch anything, I must have just flicked through them whilst I was channel hopping" "yes sir", came the reply "but you spent 36 minutes flicking through Mother's I'd like to fuck and 42 minutes flicking through whoops I've wet my panties".

Chris Catterson reckons it was the quickest he's ever seen anyone move over ten yards whilst getting 20 euro's out of his wallet at the same time.

Corky said later that the receptionist couldn't have said it any louder if he'd had a fucking loud haler.

One of my best mates Bernie Arms sent me this next section. Bernie unfortunately is keeping her Majesty Company for eight years; he is well into the second year after the Police raided his house and found a few guns and some other stuff that didn't best please them. He as been a City fan like most of us since his youth, the section is just a snippet of some his memories from the early days.

I often think back to the times when we first met in the seventies, one occasion sticks out when we went to Fulham. We loaded up the bus with crates full of flagons, so many in fact the bus aisle was packed and you had to climb over them to get up and down the aisle. One idiot on the bus was a lad called Melvyn Llewellyn, he always wore a three quarter length grey type flashers mack; his hair was greased and swept over with a wide side parting and he looked like the keyboard player in Sparks.

Well every time he asked someone to pas him a drink, the person would shake the can or bottle so much that when he opened it, the spray went everywhere, mostly over his trousers which he later took off to try and dry them on the bus window , this plan was working well until someone chucked them out of the sun roof on the M4.

When we got to Fulham he jumped off the bus and didn't notice whilst walking up the high street that someone had sprayed CCFC in big white paint down the back of his flashers mack.

He crossed the road from us because we were winding him up so much and he looked a right sight, Sparks hair cut, Woolworth sunglasses, a grey flashers mack with CCFC painted in foot high letters down the back, trouser less and wearing a pair of ox blood twenty two hole Doc Martens.

When he left us in a pub to go and find café for some grub, he came back panting for breath ten minutes later having been chased by in his words at least four separate gangs of lads, and he couldn't understand how they realised he wasn't a local. Happy days!

Gwyn, Corky and Sam Hammam

Chapter 6
The politics involved

One of my main aims when putting this book together was to catalogue some of the "politics" that took place behind the scenes. I also wanted to capture some of the fun we had during this period, whilst not ignoring some of the serious issues and risks involved in being a Cardiff City fan.

These events could sometimes be rewarding, sometimes farcical and some times so frustrating I wanted to jump out of my chair and chin someone. Some of the worst people to deal with were people involved in so called safety advisory groups. These could be made up of Councillors, local business representatives, the fires service, Health and safety officials' etc. etc.

With so many busybodies putting their noses in at times, it's a miracle football gets played anywhere at any time in this country. It does concern me with regard to management speak and thought such as "risk assessment" and "care of duty" and when I heard the phrase "delivery of the package" used in reference to the expected arrival time of our fans, I couldn't believe what I was hearing.

Fuck me, living life is full of risks and if you choose to do nothing, then nothing happens. The best way to make sure nothing goes wrong, is to do nothing. It worries me that when the slightest thing goes wrong, we have a knee jerk reaction to it. I often use the phrase using a sledge-hammer to crack a peanut.

It often appears that whilst society itself is deteriorating with regard to family values and moral responsibility, football is seen as an easy target and is targeted to be cleaner than society itself.

A lot of these people were on a real power trip, some of them little more than jumped up clerks but they had the power to put a spanner in the works if they so wished.

One club that deserves its safety council and police force is Wolverhampton Wanderers. They all deserve one another. A marriage made in Hell so to speak. Most city fans will remember the total ban placed on them in 2006. The build up to this ban didn't happen overnight however and the build up to events started some two seasons earlier.

Now due to the closeness in distance between our two clubs and remembering that anywhere within or around the two hour journey times, is classed by us as a local derby. We always travel in numbers to any Midlands club and Wolves with a reputation for occasional trouble, would ensure that any of ours looking for a bit of action would be well up for this one.

The South Wales police and our club asked me if I'd go along with them to a pre-match meeting to see if we could make some mutually acceptable arrangements that would benefit our fans and the WMP.

The meeting took place a few weeks before the game and was held in one of the hospitality suites in Molineux.

Now I knew and so did our police and our club if truth be told, that our members would have loved nothing better than to be allowed to wander about Wolverhampton town centre and fill up all the pubs by 11am, if they were given half a chance and dealt with anything that came about as it happened. The potential for some real disorder was written all over this one.

Now at the meeting I was asked by the chief police officer from the WMP how many coaches we could possibly bring on our own, i.e. without the 8 or 9 that the supporters club could guarantee to bring along as well.

Now at the time we were well established and I estimated that we would have possibly 24 coaches for this one and my plan was to try and get all the reps to stop outside Wolves on route for a drink. We would arrange in the next meeting what coaches would stop in what towns, e.g. we would send 4 to Bromsgrove, 4 to Worcester, 4 to Tewkesbury etc. That way we could spread them all out and not swamp any one place in particular.

These were the sort of things we would do week in week out, depending upon the area we were visiting. It had got so good that we would phone landlords in advance, ask them if we were welcome, and in most cases we had used that pub before and that they could now trust us, so they were more than pleased to have us back for the 2 hours or so and the till bursting revenue we would guarantee.

The older heads on the coaches would stop the younger hotheads from messing things up, and it was all sweet as.

Well this top copper was well impressed with this; all he could see was us keeping 1200 potential murderers out of his area until the last thing. However, what I did ask for was a bit of common sense, as between us and the supporters club we would be bringing over 30 bus loads to the game.

Now often you'd have the situation where they would meet the first coach as it got near the area and keep them in a lay by until the last coach arrived. Now, this could mean a delay of over an hour on many occasions. Yes it did enable the police to escort one huge convoy in together, but the down sides were the frustrations and anger it would create amongst fans stuck waiting in some lay bye, and also having 30 or so coaches arrive together at the ground causing huge queues and potential problems at the turnstiles.

What I asked for was the coaches to be taken in as they more or less arrived, but in groups of say a half a dozen or so. He thought about this and saw the benefits and it suddenly became his idea, but who cares as long as it was done.

Then came the ten million dollar question, "would they be prepared to turn a blind eye to lads hiding drink under the coaches for the journey home?" Well the look on his face you'd have thought I'd asked would he mind letting me have sex with his wife at half time. He was horrified (mind you his wife didn't look too happy either when I approached her at 3.45pm a few weeks later).

"Oh my God" he replied there was no way we could allow that to happen and it would be over his dead body. So I the replied "no problem, but the estimate I gave you earlier for 24 coaches of Valley Rams, will now be nearer five or six". Well this was quite apparently seen by him as a threat (more on that later) but I was telling it as it was. Whatever I agreed on up here, I had to then take back and sell to our members. We couldn't force them on the buses, we couldn't insist they travel with us.

I was always aware that unless we could offer something that attracted our members, they would always choose to do their own thing, there was a level of loyalty to us, but their main loyalty was to themselves and ensuring they had a good swig on the day in question.

The cost and convenience of travelling with us was a big factor, the fun and safety in numbers was another, but being able to have a drink on what was their day off was a major part of it. Now what this copper couldn't understand was if they couldn't have a drink with us and the controls we provided to some extent, then they'd either jump on trains or use cars vans and mini buses and be waiting outside the front doors of pubs in Wolverhampton from 10.30am onwards.

I wasn't making threats, I genuinely went to these meetings to try and help to limit the possibility of problems taking place, I wanted our boys to have a great day out, I also didn't want to see any of them get hurt or arrested, I didn't want any more bad press for our club and our fans, we were all supposed to be working together to try and change things.

The WMP Chief copper turned to Simon Insole and I think it may have been Richie Weber the other of our FIO's that were present but their faces more or less confirmed I was telling it how it was.

Now in all fairness to our coppers, they'd kept out of things and as I had seen in other meetings they were there to offer advice if asked, they were there to share information, but never once did I see or hear them try and tell officers from another force how to deal with us. My God, does anyone think they'd be that naïve to walk into another area and tell them how to run their operation?

Actually sometimes I wished they had been allowed to tell other forces, we may have made more progress then.

I would often say but a little tongue in cheek, let the South Wales Police travel up with say 20 Officers and keep on track with us up, back home and during the match and you can reduce the number of home officers needed by 50%. Let our coppers police us, because they know everyone, they know how to deal with people and most lads thought of them as fair in most cases. That didn't mean you could take the piss or get away with things, far from it, Simon especially knew all the tricks. We couldn't believe how often he would pop up in the middle of things just before a little kick off took place. (Fuck me up in Spurs a few years earlier, I thought they'd cloned him, he was everywhere).

Also, and usually but not in all cases, if you saw Simon or one of the other regular coppers attached to us, pulling someone for a bollocking or even arresting them, whereas in other cases this would attract a crowd all shouting "he ain't done nuffing" or" what's your name and number?" Now in most cases you'd know the lad must have been out of order or he wouldn't be having a bollocking.

Now as I'd explained these lads intending to travel to Wolves would have had a drink whatever the scenario, if you kick off the game at 8am, they'll simply spend the night before in their pubs and rather than go home for a kip they'll stay out on the lash and just get on the bus at 5 or 6am or whatever crazy time they imposed on us. Now I'm not going to try and justify this mentality and as far as I'm personally concerned whilst I like a good drink, it isn't essential to my watching football. But to some it is and whilst it doesn't make it right, it also doesn't make it wrong. It's just how it is and we're all different.

Football fans belong to a broad cross section of society and it really pisses me off when one section or other thinks they have a divine right to watch a game in hand picked circumstances and be surrounded only by people that fit into their image of how a football fan should look and act.

One of the many factors that appeal to me about the whole football thing is the mixture of people that take part. I think its great seeing an old man or woman shouting their heads off or leaping (well perhaps leaping is too strong a word) out of their seat when their team score.

Yes, I can understand why a man with a young family doesn't want to be stuck in the middle of a group of, off their face lunatics, but I can also understand why a mad well oiled young man doesn't want to be stuck in the middle of a load of families having to watch every word he utters in case he offends anyone. But there are ways around this and football should and can with some planning work around and encompass all these factors, family stands, singing areas, pop and crisp buses, lads buses, everyone should be able to enjoy themselves whilst still being safe and relaxed.

However if you read some of the football message boards and I'm sure it happens at all clubs not just in Cardiff, you'd swear that only certain individuals should be allowed to watch a game. Now I'd like to think I'm pretty fair minded and comfortable in different situations, but on some of the buses I organised for travel, whilst ten of the lads on board may have been some of my best mates and another twenty may have been friendly acquaintances, another ten may have been total strangers to me, ten others may have been people who I thoroughly disliked and I'm sure if they lived in my street or drunk in my pub, I'd be scrapping with them on a yearly basis.

Now for match day at least we were all Cardiff City fans and as long as everyone played within our rules (of which there weren't that many) then we'd all get along nicely. However if some of them didn't know how to behave and fucked around, there were plenty of good ones around to sort them out.

If anything, rather than influence good people so to speak into behaving badly or getting into trouble, I am convinced it helped a few of the dodgier ones to come more in line and to see that they could have a good day out without having to burn a pub down.

Whilst the police and the so called establishment and governing bodies had their own sets of laws and rules, so did we, but possibly not as rigid.

The vast majority of people know how they should behave and whilst they may break a few rules and regulations, you would not consider them criminals or law breakers. However my favourite rule is to use a bit of common sense, whilst the jobs worth approach just for the sake of it drives me nuts.

Often a copper will have to do what he's told by his commanding officer. The officer may know it's a load of bollocks, but it isn't his decision, he just has to carry out his orders, if things go wrong then the officer can't get the blame and the buck has to stop with old five pips on £200,000 a year.

Many is the time a decent copper will say to you "look lads I know its crap but I have to follow orders" how can you argue with that? He's just telling you how it is, how many boys would be prepared to put their career on the line just to let you through a cordon to get back to your car, even if it means walking an extra mile around rather than the twenty yards across the road. I can accept it when a copper holds his hands up and says sorry lads but that's how it is. It may be crap, but I've got to do what I'm told, rather than the other police approach which is to push or hit you simply because they can't articulate the situation to you properly.

I have done a bit of door work in my younger days and others who have worked the doors will say the same. If you are told people with trainers or jeans can't come in, then they can't come in. If you want to get paid at the end of the night, then you follow orders. That doesn't mean you have to be rude or a twat to everyone you turn away, talk to them first and then be a twat if they don't listen.

It can be very frustrating for all parties involved and I try to avoid getting into those types of situations, especially if I've had a drink, because usually there are no winners and let's be honest when you've had a drink, you have all the answers, don't you?

Now whilst that could be described as a job's worth situation, being in the police force is similar to being in the army and it really is more than your job's worth to disobey orders.

What I would describe as a job's worth situation is one such as happened to me at Old Trafford some 15 years ago. Wales were due to play England in the Rugby League World cup semi final. It gave me the chance to go along and see the much improved Old Trafford. In my wildest dreams I could never picture the day when we may be there watching Cardiff play Man U in the Premier League, mind you now it doesn't seem like such a pipe dream and more a distinct possiblity.

Anyway, I planned this one well. I was taking Beefy and his well used wheelchair up along with my six year old son. I had reserved seats in the disabled section and booked a place in the disabled car park directly opposite the stadium. They had sent me stickers to put in the window and even a map with directions.

I turned up on the day at the car park entrance only to be met by Job's worth of the year. He checked my registration against his list, then he checked my documentation against his list then he walked around the car looking it over as if I was trying to smuggle drugs into the country, checked my tax but didn't quite ask for my log book and M.O.T. but I'm sure you'll get the picture.

Anyway, he finally gave me permission to move my vehicular transport to the allocated parking slot that had been allotted to us by the club and to ensure that I parked within the designated lines highlighted or I may have my vehicle removed by the company appointed to carry out such duties if any such misdemeanours took place. Well Beefy was pissing himself and I was just sitting there trying to keep my neck wound in.

We got to our spot (or rather that designated area that had be allotted to us)

Beefy jumped in the chair and we were off. I half expected the wheelchair to get put through a scanner as we left, but there wasn't one there (though I bet he had one on order).We stopped just outside the entrance at a burger van and ordered some grub, my lad who was a typical 6 year old some how cut his hand on the ring pull off his can of coke, hardly life threatening but worthy of a sticking plaster.

I asked Beefy to keep an eye on him whilst I popped back to the car and got a plaster from my first aid kit. Well Job's worth was straight back on my case. "Can I help you?" he shouted, as I walked past his machine gun tower. Yes" I said "you can" and I carried on walking, well he was trotting on behind me now "Can I help you?" he repeated. "Yes you can" I replied. "Follow me". Well he was on the hook like a fish now. He followed me to the car, I opened the boot got a plaster out of the first aid kit and he said again "Can I help you?" but this time in his most authoritative voice, Again I said "yes, you can carry this back for me" and I gave him the plaster.

Well he carried the plaster between his finger and thumb and followed me as I marched out of the car park. He was tottering on behind me thinking what the fuck am I doing, but too dull to realise I was taking the piss out of him. I turned when I got to the gate, I took the plaster off him and thanked him for his help and walked off leaving him with a look on his face I'll never forget.

In most cases and I'm sure you'll agree it's not so much what people say, but its more a case of how they say it. Tone can be everything; a simple pleasant request can sound like a command if it is said in the wrong tone.

My approach in such situations is to start off civilly and friendly and if the person you are talking to responds badly, then let them have it both barrels, mistaking nice for soft is a lesson learnt painfully sometimes.

Back to the Wolverhampton situation, and the land of the job's worth's to beat all job's worth's.

The chief copper in the meeting was in a bit of a pickle now, he was being offered an option that would help to prevent problems by ensuring that the vast majority of travelling fans would be prepared to come on coaches and comply to any sensible regulations that were acceptable. The problem was accepting that we were in a meeting rather than a lecture and meetings tend to involve an all party discussion and input and some times negotiations with a little bit of give and take.

Now in a lecture, it's more a case of sit down and I'll tell you how it is. This copper just couldn't get his head around the fact that this was a negotiation not a lecture, and there had to be some give and not just all take. We were allowed by law to stop on route for a drink as long it was ten miles or so away from the stadium. We were allowed to enter the city limits for a drink on a coach as long as it wasn't a couple of hours before kick off and if we wanted to make our own way up and get into the city centre in dribs and drabs, then we could. I don't know what he thought he was giving us, because up until then it was only things to suit them.

Now, surely allowing the buses to have a few slabs underneath for a homeward drink was less of a threat than having thousands of us doing our own thing, with some staying in Wolves for a post match drink or stopping in any of the surrounding towns and villages on the route home. You'd think they'd be glad to get us out of there.

Now in the early part of this meeting, their officers had already voiced their concerns over their own fans behaviour. Apparently the Wolves "risk element" as they referred to them had been getting more and more active recently and were rubbing their hands at the chance of having a pop at our lot.

They went on to say that they'd had trouble at both the recent home games, I believe against, Wigan and Preston. On both games in question the Wolves fans had come down the hill after the game had finished, mingled in with the away fans walking back to the coaches. Lots of fights had broken out, but lots of families and "normals" had been a big part of the away support but they were all seen as fair game by Wolves finest. The WMP's words not mine.

Well in my naivety I thought that would be easy to stop, why not just stop the Wolves fans from walking down the hill towards the away fans, why not keep the away fans in the ground for ten minutes or so until they had cleared the streets. Why not even bring the coaches outside the away section or even move them a little closer to the stadium.

I said there'd be no problems asking our fans to stay in the stadium, whilst they cleared the streets and we would spread the word and tell our lads, it made sense and to expect it. We were quite used to such things and quite compliant if it was handled properly.

But every suggestion that we came up with was shot down. Freedom of movement, human rights, safety of crowd control, lots of excuses why they couldn't hold us in the ground and yet when they want to impose their way upon you its funny that they can dig up or invent laws on the spot to stop you doing anything they so wish. Very frustrating and another example of the unlevel playing field we so often found ourselves on.

Common sense prevailed for the pre match Wolves planning, I think the police had so many problems dealing with their own fans and the few hundred of ours that would be doing their own thing regardless, because no matter how much fun we could have on the coaches, some people still preferred to do their own thing, and that was great, but because of the amount of "lads" that travelled with us, the independent travellers were in much smaller numbers.

So we were allowed to stick to the plan we agreed on, regardless of these plans. The police still insisted on searching every bus and telling each driver with drink on board they may get reported, even though we'd agree to this and told them which buses would have drink on them. i.e. all of ours and none of the supporters club, but they searched theirs as if they had to check anyway.

There were no incidents of disorder with the crowds that had come on the buses, but that didn't stop the WMP picking out a few targets for easy arrest. You know the drunk and disorderly or abusive behaviour charges they chuck around like confetti. Mind you of the sixteen or seventeen fans that were arrested during the day for events before and after the game, when these lads got to court I believe only one was actually found guilty and all others were either found innocent or had their cases thrown out of court.

Ironically the next year almost the same number were arrested and that year of the fifteen arrested, only one was convicted and that was for throwing a pie at a copper who was bashing someone over the head with his staff.

At least this shows the judges involved in the Wolverhampton courts are switched on with regard to the methods of the world famous WMP, but I'm sure some of these factors simply add to the hatred the WMP have for us. Mind you perhaps we shouldn't take it personally, because clubs from all over the country feel the same about them.

One of the cases that got thrown out of court is worth a mention. The chap who was arrested phoned me the next day apologising for bring any shame on us (ah love him) but I could tell from his call that this chap was a decent bloke with no track record for trouble.

Now, his story went that he'd worked the night shift before the Wolves game, got straight on the bus. He had four cans on the way up and then another five pints in the pub when they stopped for an hour on route. He said he'd had no grub and was knackered and when he got off the bus in Wolves his legs had gone. He admits to being drunk and when he got off the bus rather than try and get in the game, he asked the driver could he go back on the bus to sleep it off.

Now one of the coppers saw him getting back on the bus, followed him on and then arrested him and charged him with drunk on entry into a football stadium. Fuck me, he was on the bus which was parked more than half a mile from the stadium.

The judge went mental when this got to court and really slammed the WMP and the CPS for allowing this case to go that far, and all the costs associated with it.

There were many such Mickey Mouse charges and yet when the real trouble kicked off after the game, these coppers were nowhere to be seen for the first five minutes when they were needed to do some real police work.

The game was electric. For a lot of us it was the first time back at the modernised Molineux and the atmosphere amongst our lot was spot on and made all the better with a great victory for us.

Now when the game ended, lots of us stayed behind to applaud the team who'd come over to the pitch side to acknowledge the supporters. Some of the fans had started leaving in dribs and drabs rather than pouring out en masse.

Now suddenly we became aware that something was going on outside so the vast majority who had stayed behind started now to pour out in numbers.

What we witnessed was pandemonium. There were less than a handful of coppers there and loads of Wolves fans who'd come down the hill, lots of them somehow carrying and throwing those temporary type of fence panels the police had placed all over the roadside.

Well the next few minutes were great fun, and I make no apologies for saying that. I hate bullies and what I had seen was bullying at its worse.

The majority of the Cardiff fans who had been caught up in all the initial trouble were families, and whilst the majority of "normal and family fans" hate the soul crew type image and tag that goes with our club. It was apparent later from message board postings and letters to the newspapers that even the most anti hooligan fan was glad to have the protection of our so called "hoolies" to protect them, because the police that day were clueless.

We knew this was a trouble hotspot and had been a flash point at Wolves last two home games, so why wasn't it policed accordingly? Were they hoping we'd have a hammering or possibly the Wolves risk element would be taught a lesson? Either way I don't think they were prepared for what came about.

Now the message we had been trying to get out there to our fans was don't go looking for trouble, but if you are attacked then stick together. This attack was like receiving a green light to go, and go they did.

Now I deliberately don't want to glorify violence or do the usual hoolie book stuff where my dad's bigger and harder than your dad.

When two parties are involved in such incidents, in my experience, when one group gets unstuck and takes a hammering, the reports go along the lines of, it wasn't our real lads, just a load of barmies, we didn't have the numbers and all our main faces were bubbled up by the police, but the best one and the one I love hearing, was it was no-one got the upper hand and it was honours even.

Well this was the story coming form the Wolves sections over the next few weeks. Possibly getting battered back up the hill and scattered all over the place was part of a tactical retreat to regroup for further assaults, is viewed as honours even, but those that were there know the truth and no amount of fabrication will change things.

As far as I was concerned it was a case of a load of bully boys becoming unstuck and I had no sympathy for any of those who had a slap, they came looking and got caught out.

After this incident they had a post match meeting and one of the observers present who was part of the Football League's appointed ground safety panel and a former high ranking police officer before he retired, said that it was the worse police operation he'd ever seen at a football match. Yet another reason for the close bond (NOT) between our fans, and the whole Wolves and WMP cesspit.

All these events brought even more shame and embarrassment to the WMP. The message of support we received from clubs all around the country and many from the Wigan and Preston fans who corroborated the same sort of attacks and crap policing that had occurred identically with them a few weeks earlier. We new this would lead to some form of pay back in the future for or fans and club.

The following year's fixture came along and there was no negotiating and very little communication. A bubble match was imposed on us. (yet another) A lot of us feel our club should have done more in these circumstances to refuse the bubble type arrangements, but the more level headed amongst us new the club were in a difficult position.

If they refused to accept the bubble and we demanded our full allocation with no restrictions, then that would have led to possible chaos and even more restrictions (but they came about anyway).

What I personally think would have happened is the WMP plus the Wolves tactical retreat squad would have been well up for a bit of payback and the headlines and media coverage yet again would pick on the easy targets and blame us yet again.

We would then be looking at total bans and possibly not just at Wolves. So with our numbers restricted to only 1,500 and everyone being made to travel on a bubble bus, i.e. no independent travel, and having to exchange your vouchers on the bus for tickets at the allotted rendezvous point.

Now we knew they were out for arrests and to make us look bad, so we ensured that everyone followed the rules to the letter of the law. What we said to our members is that it would spite and annoy the WMP if they could find no reason or excuse to arrest any of our fans or turn a whole coach back home because they found one can of lager under a seat. By taking this approach, the lads felt as though they were getting one over on them and played along.

We made sure we had loads of video and still cameras in evidence to make them aware we were gathering our own evidence and this pissed them off even more. They did their best to antagonise and wind people up but no one was biting. The instructions they had sent out for a rendezvous point were even wrong and we were told to meet just off junction 2 on the M5, which would have been the most direct route and the route you would take if you drove up in a car. But what they meant to write was just off junction 2 on the M54, only a slight misprint so they said and one that could have caused chaos if we hadn't clocked what they were playing at and phoned everyone on route to make sure they went to the correct one. Yes a genuine mistake by the WMP, make your own minds up.

The match had got to half time with no problems and with 5 minutes to go to half time people started making their way down to the concourse for some refreshments. Now before the game they had opened the bars and served alcohol with no problem, the shutters opened at half time and everyone's happy.

Suddenly after serving the first twenty or so with another fair few seeing their plastic pint glasses being filled, the bar manager storms in behind the bar and tells the staff they shouldn't be serving alcohol at half time and pulled the shutters down.

Well it was pandemonium, some people had been served and were waiting for change, some were half served and there were loads more queuing to get served and then being told the bar was shutting. All of a sudden a chant goes up "we want beer, we want beer". Some of the lads at the front were shaking the now closed shutters. It was all a bit boisterous but never threatening and if someone like Simon our FIO had been allowed to come down and speak to the lads, it would have been over in seconds, instead this was just the excuse needed and the outside doors swung open and dozens of robbo cops in full body armour came pouring through the packed concourse.

Now this concourse wasn't just full of boozed up lads looking for more booze, there were all sorts there, a real broad section of our fans, if anything when we have a bubble match imposed on us, the amounts of "up for it lads" reduces and the die hard never miss a match. "Normal's" and family fans therefore become a bigger percentage of the travelling support.Well they were all fair game for it today, people were just knocked over or pushed out of the way, anyone complaining was getting struck by batons, and it was game on. These are exactly the flash points and situations we try and prevent from starting; because once they start they just spread like wild fire.

One thing that is sad really, but can work in our favour after events have taken place is when people who are the salt of the earth type fair minded people recount events, and when judges and authority figures get to hear evidence and statements from such people, then it does carry more clout, than just having the versions of events from what people see us stereo typical hoolies or lads.

Just as had happened the year previously when these fans had come under attack from the Wolves fans, when you have people in professions such as teaching and even legal backgrounds, some elderly and retired all singing from the same hymn sheet and with all the stories matching, well there were plenty of stories that came about from what happened over the next ten minutes or so and most of them had a common denominator, the police were out of control and a situation that could have been solved diplomatically, was now almost a full scale riot.The police's master plan it would appear was to batter everyone in the concourse area, and then push them all back up through one set of entry steps, even though they had entered the concourse through four different entrances. This now led to hundreds of people being pushed back into one aisle with nowhere to go, the seats adjacent to the aisle in most cases had people already sitting in them, now the police were trying to get another few hundred into a space that didn't exist.People were falling over seats, falling down in the aisles and getting whacked for their trouble as well. People near the front had to spill onto the pitch side to escape the problems. This only made things worse and police now came along the pitch side forcing these people back into the already packed trouble area.Now most of the people who were seeking refuge on the pitch side were the vulnerable older and younger fans amongst us, kids were crying an elderly people were trying to remonstrate with officers who were having none of it.The top half of the book cover illustrates this situation and you can see the aisles full of baton wielding coppers lashing out at anyone in reach. The reporters and commentators made mention of these events and we were glad that independent people could see what was taking place.

I don't want to labour on and detail to much more on this incident, there are many chapters in other Cardiff based books which have covered events of that day, but suffice to say we were held up as the guilty party, an enquiry was called for and every supporter and supporter's representative along with our clubs management welcomed this, we seen it as the ideal and fair way to get some justice and truth behind events.But surprisingly yet again another enquiry did not get off the ground, things like this were happening to us yearly it seemed, we had been promised an enquiry two years running for events that took place in Huddersfield.What I thing is more likely the case is when people sit down in the cold light of day and start looking at details, they realise they are opening a can of worms, and that they will be asked to justify their actions, which of course they would find embarrassing and even dangerous. For example the Wolverhampton situation could have led to another Hillsborough disaster with people getting crushed and trampled, the safety of the general public should be the major concerns of these officers, and yet it was them who nearly caused another disaster.

Whilst we didn't get our enquiry, we did have another fifteen fans arrested and taken to court, with all these cases bar one getting acquitted or thrown out of court, with the judge apologising in some cases for wasting people's times and tax payer's money.One lad was convicted and found guilty of throwing a pie at and officer who the lad seen striking an elderly gentleman with his baton.This trouble that no one had bothered to analyse and fairly apportion the blame to lead to us having a total ban from next years game. That ban caused them so much embarrassment and our fight against the injustice achieved national exposure and the full support of the Football Supporters Federation (F.S.F.)

One of our fans Steve (Dayo) Day came up with a plan to hire a hot air balloon and to have it fly and hover above Molineux whilst the game was played, thus allowing the fifteen or so Cardiff fans on board to beat the ban.

The press loved this story and it led to the press looking deeper into the reasons for this total ban on our fans. Unfortunately the weather that day meant the balloon could not take to the skies, but the desired publicity had been achieved, and they were having one hell of a job to brush things under the carpet.

Now facts and figures or statistics even, can be used both ways. Politicians are especially well known for using such figures to prove a point, whilst we all new that often these figures didn't paint the full picture.Well now it was our turn to play politician. When Vince or myself got interviewed by any media agency, we would use the conviction figures of one conviction only for the past two seasons games, and we would go on to say that whilst we agreed that even one arrest was too many, one man convicted for throwing a pie should hardly warrant a full ban.We would also ask for some consistency and play the racist card! "Why only us?" we would ask, "Is it because we are Welsh?" were they now saying that any club visiting them and subsequently having a fan arrested, would then have a total ban imposed on them as well.The police could point fingers and say there had been loads of disorder, but the facts were, only one person had been convicted at each game, my God there had been double figures of home arrests amongst the Wolves fans at both these games, did that mean they were going to shut Molineux and lock out all the home fans.

Its all total bollocks, you don't ban every customer from entering Tesco's because 1% of them may shoplift, no you set about firstly making it difficult for anyone to shoplift and then put in measures to catch those that do then punishing them severely to make an example of them.The U.K. could end shoplifting in one week by bringing out a law stating that anyone found guilty of shoplifting would be shot by firing squad, fuck me you'd only after see them shooting one person to cure the worse case of kleptomania amongst the whole population. (Mind you I hope they don't take up this idea and apply it to football).It may seem mad, and it is, but so is punishing everyone because of one or two knob heads causing problems.Anyway suffice to say I don't think Jez Moxey the knowledgeable football genius American chairman of Wolves will be pushing for a total ban this year. He took so much flak, even off Wolves fans who don't want to watch football without having away fans present. Also just to put the icing on the cake in the four seasons whilst Moxey as been at Wolves they have yet to beat us at Molineux and I'd like to think all the fuss he's created as acted as a motivation to our players to up their game.

Dibbs (ex Valley Ram Rep) continues to take coaches away after the fall of the Rams

Martyn, Wolf, and the Port Talbot Rams

Chapter 7
Help from above

Within the very first few months of starting up the Valley Rams, it was apparent that our initial target of setting up a small travel club with no other political aims or aspirations to change the way football fans were treated in general had moved on to another level. The numbers of people travelling with us ensured that on a regular basis we were now taking 15 plus coaches to away games. Our membership was growing week by week and we had obviously created something that was different to your "typical" supporters club.One of our problems was that we were re-writing the rule book slightly, but I felt that whilst we had the help and support of our club and our local police to a fair extent. We needed help from higher places if we were to achieve any real change. One thing that helped convince me to carry on the route we had chosen was an interview I heard on Talk Sport one day whilst on my way to work.

I can't recollect which match or which country England had been playing the week previously but more trouble had occurred, again between the England fans and the police of whichever country was involved. This was the main topic for debate on that morning show. Suddenly they introduced someone who I hadn't heard of previously but who has since become a close personal friend and a trusted advisor on so many occasions. This person was introduced on the radio as a Doctor Clifford Stott who was a lecturer in psychology in Liverpool University.

When I first heard him being introduced my initial reaction was here goes they've wheeled out another academic with his head stuck up his arse. But I couldn't have been more wrong. What he went on to say was so refreshing and enlightening that it was the shot in the arm I needed to give me the final push in the direction that I went on to take. Cliff, I found out from listening that morning and further inquiries that I went on to make had done many academic papers and studies and presentations on such things as crowd control, crowd dynamics and many football related topics. He was now being employed on an ad hoc basis by the Home Office to look into football related issues which had mainly come about from the image of England fans abroad.

Now some of the things that I picked up from this interview were Cliff's approach to interaction between the fans and the police. One of the key points was if you police a situation with aggressive Robocop type police rather than prevent problems, often this creates an aggressive atmosphere which invariably leads to problems.

The Rise and Fall of the Cardiff City Valley Rams

Cliff's message was to build on a relaxed atmosphere with interaction, have low profile officers in short sleeved shirts and no helmets, just mixing with fans and helping the situation whilst monitoring any possibility of change amongst the crowds present. Obviously if fans had gone there intent on looking for trouble they would have to be dealt with and if this meant an aggressive police response then so be it.

But what had happened so many times previously was the small hard core of hooligans intent on causing trouble would lead to everyone present becoming involved and caught up in such events. Now this was something as a fan I was well aware of and it was particularly representative of what occurred with Cardiff city fans on a weekly basis. What Cliff was saying was if you treat the vast majority of fans fairly and create the right atmosphere, the minority element would become isolated and lose the back up of the crowds which invariably had been caught up in so many events in the past. When I heard someone of Cliff's standing talking so much sense, it reassured me that we weren't fighting a lone battle. When I got into work that day, I did try to trace Cliff by ringing Liverpool University to make contact, but it was in between terms and he wasn't available to take my calls for the next few weeks or so. This led to my contacting Cliff being put on the back burner so to speak and invariably forgotten about until I met him in person by chance the following year.This meeting with Cliff was not planned and came about in a service station coach park just south of Leeds. It was our first visit to Elland Road for many years and after the infamous FA cup match with Leeds the year previously, to say that things were tense would be a massive understatement. The match was allocated to be a "bubble" match, that was of no surprise to us and if truth be told a match that needed a "bubble" to allow the game to go on without major violence. I was concerned as an organiser that innocent fans could get assaulted and injured if they had been allowed to travel up under their own steam. Every Cardiff fan was seen as fair game by the vast majority of Yorkshire not just Leeds United fans. Hate is a very strong word and shouldn't be used in football terms but it's the only word that would describe the feelings held for us by most Leeds fans. The police had major concerns, they knew they would have their hands full stopping the Leeds fans from attacking us at any opportunity they could and the last thing they needed was a few thousand of us being allowed to travel freely around Leeds looking after ourselves and the chaos that would have caused.

This led to the police wanting and needing to get us on board and whilst I didn't go as far as asking them to find us allocated pubs in the Leeds area, what I did ask them to do was to take a light hearted non aggressive type of approach at the RV point and in all fairness to them they did this and it created the right mood amongst our fans. Little things can make or break such days. A little bit of over zealous policing would have created an aggressive response from our fans, whilst a bit of friendly banter between the two parties got things off to a good start.

Whilst I was in the car park meeting the buses as they came in, and trying

Frankie Humphries and some of the Doe a Deer crew

Frankie Mason's Cwmbran Army

Time for a drink in the services

The Rams on their travels

Insane Wayne and Alfie

Keeping an eye on proceedings

Who ate all the pies? Me, Jumbo, Wayne and Ali

Wolves away. Ugly bus arrives at Wolves

The Holyhead lads, much travelled

The Rams at the last ever league game at Ninian Park ~ April 25th 2009

The Rams at the last ever league game at
Ninian Park ~ April 25th 2009

The Rams at the last ever league game at Ninian Park ~ April 25th 2009

to keep everyone happy. Nashy (Wayne Nash, Cardiff City's stadium manager), called me one side and said "Gwyn, I've got someone I'd like you to meet" and he introduced me to Cliff Stott. I felt like I was meeting an old friend even though until now we had never made contact. I recounted the story of listening to his radio interview and that helped to cement our relationship even further. Cliff had been asked to attend this match by the Home Office and the Football Association. He was well aware of some of the things we'd organised at the Rams and it was ticking a lot of the right boxes. These events would lead to him attending dozens more Cardiff matches and producing an academic study, using a lot of events and experiences gathered form his time amongst us. Using my limited knowledge of psychology but vast experience of what made our fans tick, prior to the Leeds match during the meetings we had had organising this game, the message that I was putting over to our fans was the best way to have an off the field victory at Leeds was to come away with no arrests, no further tarnishing of our reputation and to prove to the watching world that if you are treated properly we would behave properly.

The people of Leeds and a lot of media involved would have liked nothing better than for us to live up to this image and vision they had given us as being third world mindless savages. I believe that if we had played up to that image or given any justification of that view it would have led to us either having total restrictions on travelling to away matches or even points being deducted. This was a chance for our fans to show that we truly supported our club and that we wanted to help and we were all in it together. The supporters club also played their part in this day's events. One of their great ideas was to lay a wreath in commiseration at the tragic loss of the Leeds fans that had been killed in Turkey. It was agreed that we could lay this wreath at the base of the Billy Bremner statue outside Elland road. This was done for genuine reasons to show we should all be united against such acts of violence and that as football fans whilst rivalry and banter is very much a part of things, this should never lead to violence especially at the tragic cost of lives as had happened in this case.

These plans had achieved a bit of positive publicity in the Leeds press and whilst it didn't convince all of the Leeds fans that we came in peace, it may have helped to convince some of their fans that we were not as bad as we were made out to be. It was ironic that whilst we were laying the wreath, many of their fans were being held back by security fencing applauded us, whilst others were still giving us the "Fuck off back to Wales, you sheep shagging bastards welcome" This almost led to the Leeds fans fighting amongst themselves.

Whilst as there is with all our away games, there will always be a number of younger hotheads who often feel invincible because they have the protection of the older element plus the large numbers that we take. Sometimes many of us feel the younger ones should be made to go through the similar situations that we had in the past. A good hammering would have helped to remind these kids what really happens in life, part of growing up should teach you that sooner or later you have to back up what you give out, lot's of the gobby kids in football are so well protected by security measures in the football world 21st century style, they think they are invincible but I doubt if any of them have actually been caught up in a real up and downer.But whilst we had a few of these type amongst us today, on the whole amongst the crowd today were a much bigger percentage of the older type battle hardened faces who will always turn out whenever they feel there is a need for a show of strength. It was funny looking at some of the coppers faces when they noticed the type of fans who were in the majority this time. So often they will be used to dealing with the teenage type chav hooligans but I think the average age of our small army surprised them more than a little.

Now one of the benefits of the communication that we had had with the police and clubs was the benefit of being able to pass communication and information on to our travelling fans either through our regular meetings or on the internet message boards. If you tell people they may well be kept in the stadium for an hour or so after the game, whilst they may moan at that particular time at least they can't say that they are surprised when it actually happens on the match day. Now the police had spoken to us about this possible one hours delay after the game and whilst I could see the need for this, what I had asked for is if they could leave us in our seats, even leave the refreshment areas open and leave the tannoy on playing a bit of music and giving us the scores of other games. They did this and it was really successful. If anything in a bizarre way it added to the great day that we had.

The result had gone our way, the atmosphere was electric and the sing song and banter we had for that hour or so will stay with me forever. One of the things I remember at this time, was three Leeds fans who must have been the last ones in the stadium walking across the seated areas towards us calling it on. It was so pathetic that it was hilarious. Instead of riling up our lads, who in previous times would have probably been ripping the fences down, all it achieved on this occasion was a major piss take with three thousand of us singing "3 boys, you've only got 3 boys". But this was capped when one of them fell sprawling over the seats, only to then hear the same three thousand boys singing the "she fell over" chant. Seeing this lad jump up on his feet as if nothing happened and then the three of them trying to save face whilst making a dignified retreat was epic. Now whilst we were held in the stadium we were more than aware of the carnage and chaos that was going on outside. And whilst if I am honest, a lot of us, and even a part of me would have liked to have been outside amongst it. I'm not going to try and justify those reasons. It's something either you have inside you or not. Those that share these feelings will understand, whilst those that have never had these feelings will never see or understand where this gut feeling/buzz comes from. Finally when they let us out into the fenced off compound where the coaches were, everyone exited the stadium in quite a relaxed manner. There was still several hundred Leeds fans who were in small pockets all around the area, but the police were more or less in control of the situation and at the end of the day, if you are a home fan it's hard to justify why you are still outside the stadium one hour or so after the match has finished. 99% of the time you are there either to witness events or be part of them. And if the police take a heavy handed approach with you, then what can you say?

One story linked to this day's events comes back to me from big Sam Murphy and I'll and try to put it in his words as I recollect.

Sam was in his local pub The Windsor in Merthyr Vale. Now the landlord Richie (the infamous one who was fined for shagging the big plastic swan at the Vetch in the mid seventies) is married to a girl from Doncaster, a big Leeds stronghold.

She had some family down visiting and amongst the family was a 40 year old chap with his 18 year old son whose left arm was bandaged. When big Sam walked into the bar for his nightly pint, Richie said to this young lad, tell Big Sam how you hurt your arm. When the lad's knees had stopped knocking, because Big Sam doesn't look like the angel of mercy in anyone's eyes, he recounted the story to Sam saying that he'd been outside Elland Road that day with a gang of his hoodie mates when a copper gave him a shove to move him on and the lad and the copper exchanged words.

The copper more or less said – "piss off home, why are you hanging around here?" And the lad replied in his best macho tones that he was waiting for the Cardiff scum to be let out. To which the copper replied "you waiting for them? There are three thousand gorillas in there waiting to rip your fucking head off. Now the best thing you can do for your own safety, is to fuck off home before we open the gates". And with that the copper gave him a final push, causing him to fall over a small wall and hurt his arm. He made sure he showed Big Sam his bandaged arm, hoping for a bit of sympathy from him, who had nearly pissed himself laughing by now. We were escorted out of the area with no real incidents, plenty of flashing the V's and cut throat gestures but otherwise nothing of note. This match led to around 35 Leeds fans being arrested either on the day or later after viewing CCTV footage. Several were jailed and many had football bans. We were commended by the police, the press and the Leeds club for our behaviour and cooperation. In my eyes that was a far bigger victory for all of us, victories in the past often centred around us getting the upper hand in some scrap etc. but all that had led to was us being targeted and punished even more by the authorities.

The frustrating thing I found then and still do now, is that whilst there were many successful occasions such as this, it didn't lead to any major national changes in the approach taken to dealing with football fans. and not just ours but fans in general . Some of the things we were saying and doing such as improved communication take a friendlier approach, have pre-match discussions etc were achieving the desired results. But whilst we found we would be building bridges in one area, other areas still had a mind set that nothing would change.

It is a pity that you can't get two area police forces to have similar approaches or methods and my experience is that each force area can be slightly insular and often out on a limb in relation to other areas, with seemingly little done to make them toe the line. They all seem to be allowed to do their own

The Rise and Fall of the Cardiff City Valley Rams

thing and the interpretation of laws and how they are applied seem to depend on who the chief constable is at any particular time. An example of this, is North Wales where you have more chance of escape, if you are a murderer than a speeding driver. I recently watched an hour long programme showing the troubles involved at a Leeds United home match against Millwall. This match had trouble written all over it and the costs and logistics involved must have been astronomical. It showed 700 Millwall fans arriving at Leeds central station on a train with thousands of Leeds United risk fans hanging around the city centre awaiting their arrival.

There was a huge police presence with massive disruption to the city centre. The plan was to transport the Milwall fans on double decker coaches from the city centre to Elland Road. But this would have meant having 700 Milwall fans locked inside an empty stadium on their own for three or four hours. So the wonderful idea you'd think that they had re-invented the wheel, and we had been doing this with the Rams for the past 7 years, was to find a massive pub near the station where they could safely allow the Milwall fans to congregate whilst having a meal and a drink and other freedoms that go along with your human rights. This then makes it easier to police. You can use far fewer officers to keep 700 people in a pub especially when they are happy to be in there and it's also easier to block off a street and prevent any Leeds fans from getting within spitting distance.Problems started occurring though when these double decker coaches were being taken to the stadium. Many windows were put through by Leeds fans along this route, throwing stones and missiles at the buses and also by Millwall fans inside the coaches kicking the windows out to return fire so to speak. Apparently there was £10,000 damage done to the buses on that short journey alone. After the match Millwall fans also needed to be kept in the ground for an hour or so whilst the police tried to clear the area. Unfortunately, because of lack of communication and any pre match discussion you had a huge mob of Millwall fans locked in the stadium behind the entrance fences getting more agitated and aggressive by the minute. The police had a nightmare situation of trying to work out some way of marching these 700 fans back to the train station, which is a good few miles walk along a route where there would have been thousands of Leeds fans awaiting to attack this convoy at every opportunity.

In the end however, after much begging or possibly blackmailing the Leeds bus company who had withdrawn their double deckers, the bus company agreed to bring them back for the return journey. What I am trying to show here is that you had two similar high profile matches but because of the nature of our existence as the Valley Rams we could play a part in achieving a huge saving of police costs and damages and a match where in the police's words where they were only faced with one hostile group rather than two hostile groups as they were with the Leeds and Millwall match.

But our thanks for that seasons efforts simply resulted in us being told that next year we would have to have a bubble match, which we would have put up with, but this time with a restricted amount of fans travelling. Possibly 1500 rather than 3000 and this was more to do with restrictions called for by the Leeds Safety Advisory Group, this is a group involved at every club as I wrote earlier and here at Leeds they weren't looking to reward any Cardiff fans no matter how well behaved we'd been. So whilst the Police were singing our praises, it had no effect on the other members in this "SAG" They tried to come up with what they claimed were valid reasons for this reduction in numbers, but to us it was another kick in the teeth and seen as another punishment rather than reward and acknowledgement for any actions that we had carried out the season previously.

All this led to even more disillusionment amongst our membership and it was voted that the Rams as an organisation would not travel to Leeds and called for a boycott of sorts. In the end 265 fans from Cardiff travelled whereas the year previously we had 3,000. And just to rub salt in the wounds after this match Ken Bates the owner of Leeds United had the audacity to complain that the police costs were the same, yet the revenue from the away fans was much less and this was mostly down to his club's part in imposing the restrictions anyway.

Wolves away 2004

The Police divide us down the middle at Wolves away

Chapter 8
Not always the same enemy

Whilst the Police had usually been seen by fans as the "bad guys" and any restrictions put on us would be blamed on the Police, in truth this wasn't always the case and my genuine concern for the future of football in the U.K. is that in the near future it will be almost impossible to put a match on anywhere.I don't think that this is just a football thing either and I'll try not to get too political here, but the things that do my head in, are the Risk management and duty of care statements etc that go along with getting a match put on are now being applied at all sorts of events, charity fairs, barbecues, local concerts, local carnivals. In fact anything likely to attract a crowd of more than a few dozen (Swansea should be OK then)

The best way to avoid risk is to take no risk, and then nothing ever happens, but the risk of getting hurt is reduced. How the hell do we manage to get any of our brave young soldiers to fight wars for us and do so using well publicised unsuitable gear and being ill equipped.Yet, try putting on a football match and you'll have helicopters, riot vans and coppers in more gear than front line soldiers, and this is to allow a sporting event to take place. They'll refuse to grant a match certificate unless every steward is registered. There are laid down numbers of first aiders, there are laid down numbers of crowd control stewards, there can't be any other events within the area that may also require levels of policing that would mean one or the other being cancelled, and the problem is every so called agency involved in decision making will be fighting their own corner for their own recognition and self importance.

Another worry and we have already seen the early stages of this taking place is the costing. Who should pay for policing on match days and at what areas? There are calls now that the home club should pay for policing in club catchment areas well before and well after the games involved.As far as I was aware the clubs were responsible for police cost in the stadium area, but now they are being asked to pay for policing in the city centre and where will this stop?

The police force is run as a business (don't ask, you'd be safer investing in the British Banking set up) so as with any business the more revenue they can raise, the better it suits them. Also who will decide how many officers will be needed? If every officer allocated to football is actually earning a profit for their force then you can imagine how rapidly the officers required will rise and what this will do to the ever increasing costs already involved.

The Rise and Fall of the Cardiff City Valley Rams

But whilst these are areas of major concerns, the best place to fight these battles is from within the system and whilst lots of everyday fans will have heard of the F.S.F. few amongst us will really support this organisation, yet it is the only way to hold on to and fight for our game. The people involved at the F.S.F. contain a lot of well educated people who have a direct voice through the House of Lords and Parliament. These are where the battles need to be fought and won.

The majority of us sit back bang our chests, stamp our feet and make a noise whilst watching our beloved game being ripped from us as we breathe. Whilst possibly not wanting to get involved in organisations such as the FSF, we should all try and do our best to support such groups in any small way we can. Divide and conquer, well let's unite and defend.

We have got used to dealing with police up and down the country and are well aware of the inconsistencies that exist from area to area, but what I am seeing more and more now is an almost Para military approach by certain clubs and their stewards to all fans, but away fans in general.Now whilst we can all recall incidents of "bad policing" or stitch ups etc.What we must say is that no matter how bad it is or even unlawful, at least (not that justifies it) its being carried out by professionally well trained officers in the employ of our Government (that's what it says in the very small print, lol).We now have stewards who are less qualified than doormen acting as if they are the new enforcers at football.

Clubs like Charlton, Crystal Palace, Reading and even Crewe have stewards who think they have a new rule book. But the best ones of all, can be found at Nottingham Forest. Now the bloke in charge at the times I refer to, was a man named I believe Eddie Curtis, he was a retired ex police chief inspector (no surprises there now) he was also the head honcho for England away. The FA would use him as some sort of expert on football disorder matters.Well our first game for quite a few years at Nott'm Forest came along, we hadn't played each other for a number of years and this was seen as a possible risk match. Forest had a bit of a reputation, whilst it wasn't a new stadium so to speak it had been totally revamped and lots of us would want to go and see it.We were allowed three thousand tickets for this game and they went like hot cakes. Whilst Vince or I hadn't been invited or involved in pre match talks (it was still the very early days of our set up) our police and Nashy had held discussion and in all fairness the police took a pretty relaxed approach. They found us pubs around the stadium and the vast majority of those travelling that day went by coach and there were no problems to mention.

There was potential for trouble however and some of our more well up for it Soul Crew boys, with a large smattering of the docks boys had planned to go up in a fleet of cars and group up in the City centre. Now this had been kept really quiet. Most plans of this nature become common knowledge within days and you will find stuff on the message boards etc. but this plan had been put together with very little being known about it.Now while we were pubbed up near the ground having a swig just a few miles up the road was a convoy of thirty or forty cars and small vans making their way into the City centre.

Now I have spoken to many different lads from that convoy, and whilst it would seem that the well laid out plans had gone like clock work up until now, suddenly the first cars were getting the rush of adrenaline and could smell the trouble brewing. Apparently every time they came to a roundabout or traffic light they would lose another couple of cars. It's hard work keeping all together through city centre traffic and this convoy was now well split up.The lads in the first few cars were so gung ho and up for it I doubt if they even looked in their mirrors, but just as they got to a pub that was used by Nott's finest they could see they had been clocked. Four cars pulled into the car park and the sixteen or so lads got out expecting to be joined by the others, but were aware there was now a tidy mob coming out of the pub towards them.

They didn't have many options open to them and knowing the lads present, running away wasn't one of them. Now this is the situation they found themselves in, I'm not glorifying it or justifying it, these boys had gone there looking for it and they were happy to take what came. Now the ones coming for it weren't Saturday shoppers or shirt wearing scarfers who innocently got caught up in it, they were like minded lads out for a bit of the same, but with the numbers involved they thought they were well safe.

From what I'm told and those that know the lads wouldn't doubt it Jonathan and Nilsy got it all together rallied the troops and waited for the onslaught. Now when Forest got there I'm sure they partly expected a show and after all it *was* Cardiff, but the front line of what faced them made them stop in their tracks.

Instead of steaming into the small group, they were having to gee each other on to be first in there, and those that were, got put on their arse. I am sure our lads were hoping the back up troops would be along soon, but the only back up that came was for a dozen or so coppers, and luckily two of them were our spotters.

They got bang in the middle of things but by now there were a dozen or so Notts lads sparked out on the road and the others still trying to look the part.

More coppers came and got some order. The Notts Police went straight to our main lads (who I'm sure they had dossiers like MI5 on) they were about to arrest them when our FIO's stepped in and stuck up for them, what they said was whilst they'd come out of the scrap on top, they could hardly be arrested for defending themselves against a much bigger group.

Common sense prevailed and the boys got a let off and taken to the ground. Now whilst some may see this as our coppers sticking up for our fans, they couldn't be further from the truth. Nils and Jonathan would have been top of these coppers most wanted lists. The boys knew the score and in the near future would both get done and jailed by them for other events, but on this day they had to say it as they'd seen it, and the boys were simply defending themselves, a little too well, but none the less defending themselves. Nottingham's big hard hooligan crew responded by trashing the cars later, perhaps they thought it would help their hooligan image attacking unprotected cars, sad twats!

The Rise and Fall of the Cardiff City Valley Rams

Meanwhile at and around the stadium everything was sweet until fans started entering the ground, you could sense the tension, the stewards were really trying to impose themselves and the vast majority of them looked more like doormen than your typical club steward. The police were real cool and chatty and they had to intervene in several confrontations that were springing up due to the overzealous stewarding, everyone was searched as if you were boarding a plane to Iraq, kids elderly no one was exempted, they were really trying to impose themselves on the Cardiff city fans, the problem would occur just before kick off when the vast majority of our well oiled lads would turn up on masse, they would as always cut things fine, this meant maximum time in the pub before the game with a brisk walk to the ground and straight in, no time for arsey searches, I.D. and ticket checks.

Something had to give and in this case it was the stewards, with five minutes to kick off and six hundred or so fans surging towards the turnstiles, the stewards original plans of imposing themselves upon us and trying to intimidate this mob into an orderly compliant group wasn't working and luckily before it all got too hot, the police stepped in and more or less told the stewards to chill out and back off.

The police could see the bigger picture, and at the end of the day in such situations, they can call it as they wish and overrule anyone basically in the name of maintaining public order. This is one of those laws/rules that so often were used against us. We would be stopped from going into town centres or even leaving pubs we'd been put in and the excuse used was that we were being held there to reduce the risk of public disorder. It's one of those laws we can't win an argument against and that the Police need little justification in applying, at the end of the day, if they took the view that they were reducing the risk of public disorder, then job done as far as the law is concerned, common sense don't come into it but where do you draw the line, and in fact, is there a line to draw?

Anyway, our old pal Eddie Curtis and his para military new model army stewards were seething, their power base had been overruled, and so it was pay back time. Now for this match I believe we had been allowed three thousand tickets even though it was possible to get four thousand away fans into the away end. We were well used to these restrictions and limits being imposed on us, this had come about by a League initiative some years earlier highlighting a dozen or so clubs who would have restrictions placed on them because their fans constantly stood at away game and not only that but they would stand in front of a seat that hadn't been allocated to them, choosing to stand or sit where they wanted to and next to their own mates.

Now we'd become well used to this, but the whole nature of these restrictions were used as a "punishment" and also safety factor so they reckoned, yet whilst being punished for the way we liked to watch football, some clubs would still insist on trying to make you sit for the whole match in the allotted seats, even though our restricted numbers and punishment was an acknowledgement of the fact that we didn't anyway!!. How many punishments for one offence were being called for? Now in Forest as we entered the away end, you could see loads of empty seats netted off, and obviously the great plan was to allow three thousand seats for three thousand fans, regardless of the fact that there were thousand of empty extra seats available.

Now what would happen in most cases, was our fans would know the score, those that wanted to stand for all or most of the match would head for the back centre of whichever stand we were in, those that wanted to sit for all or most of the game, would sit in the front or the wings, everything sweet and sorted by ourselves using some good old common sense. Now in the so called name of "Ground Safety" instead of letting three thousand fans spread out and relax amongst four thousand seats, the Forest plan was, you will do exactly as we tell you, you will sit and you will sit in the seat we tell you to.

Well this was leading to chaos and again the police took charge and moved the netting allowing everything to calm down and have a good day out, everyone that is except for Edie and his troops. They couldn't let this lie, every chance they had a little snatch squad that would go in amongst the crowd and cause tension and confrontation, you'd have half a dozen bully boy stewards picking out what they thought were the easier targets amongst us, but as they soon learnt, our lot would not stand by and watch people getting picked off and bullied they'd surge over have their five pence worth forcing the stewards to back of before they got slapped.

None of this was called for, the mood amongst the fans was jovial and the only problems were being caused by jobs worth stewards who were determined to impose their petty regulations, yet the only likely danger or safety problems again the police took charge of the situation and everything calmed down with no issues.

The game finished, we all left and made our way home, there was only one arrest all day and that was for one of our young idiots shouting out a racist comment from his car window whilst driving out of the car park. Granted there could have been mayhem if the planned soul crew kick off had come off in the city centre, but in reality there had been a minor set too with no so called civilians or getting hurt or any damage to property. If truth be told we heard the Notts police were quite pleased that their so called risk element had come unstuck and had their arses slapped.

Well next years fixture soon came about and this time I was asked by our club and police to attend a joint meeting up in Nottingham. It worked out well for me because I was up in that area on family business at the time so it fitted in well with my plans. I turned up at the stadium and met our lot who introduced me to the Notts police involved, they genuinely seemed pleased to meet me, and whilst this concept of involving fans in match planning was only just starting off, they could see the benefits it could offer and had an open mind.

However, our friend Eddie Curtis was there representing the Nott's Forest club and I could tell that firstly he didn't want me there, after all why would a football fan have any say or opinion about what was after all only a football game, and not only that why did they need any sort of meeting, his type of

The Rise and Fall of the Cardiff City Valley Rams

approach was this is what will happen, this is what we will be doing, and no one should dare challenge or question us.

Now after the formality of the introductions were over, old Jobs worth was centre stage, he started off by saying the club were going to restrict our support to fifteen hundred for this years game, that meant a further reduction from the previous year of 50%. Even the police were taken aback, he went on to say they were imposing these restrictions because their game with us last year had seen the worse outbreak of football hooliganism he'd ever witnessed in all his years in football. Now let's not forget that besides for his position with the club, he was also involved with England away games and was some sort of expert of football control measures (my arse).

Well even the Notts police had to question this man's reasoning, and the inspector said that there had been no outbreaks of disorder in or around the game and went on to say they'd only had one arrest for what was basically a minor offence. He went on to say that overall the Police had been pleasantly surprised with our fans general behaviour. In fact they had already taken steps and made plans for this seasons game and they'd arranged with Notts County Football club to open up for our fans and allow us to drink and congregate there, this was a very short walk for our fans and when it came to the day, it all worked out well.

But old Edie Jobs worth's vision of football hooliganism was not in line with any one else present that day. His vision of fans walking with their heads bowed, in single file, sitting where and when they were told and not daring to question the bullyboy's approach, that's how it should work and anything else was football hooliganism at its worse!

He went onto add that he would teach these hooligans a lesson and if they didn't comply and follow out his instructions fully, then they would have further reduction of 50% for the following season, therefore reducing the away support to 750, mad and frightening that people like this had any power or position in football.

I had been biting my tongue and waiting for my chance, it was quite obvious that there would be no compromise or negotiations that would change this mans approach, he was in a position where he could impose these sanctions and he was going to, his power and control had been challenged last year by fans and police alike, and this was his chance at payback.

Their police asked me what my views were and I replied that whilst I was disappointed and didn't agree with the reasoning there was little I could do to change things, I did add that that this would give another negative message to our fans that had caused no trouble but yet again were being punished. I was concerned that our fans would blame the Nott's police rather than the Nott's Forest club but that I would bed doing my utmost to let our fans know where the blame firmly lay.

I also asked that if our fans were having such restrictions placed upon them then I hoped that Forest would now accept that this game would have to be all ticket for the home fans as well.

Eddie was back up centre stage again, "all ticket for our fans, I think not" he replied, he went on to say that in his experience, making a home game all ticket could reduce the home attendance by up to a good few thousand and that they relied heavily on the walk up audience on match days, it would cost them thousands of pounds in lost revenue. I chirped in saying that if it wasn't all ticket, then our fans that couldn't get a ticket because of the reduced allocation would simply turn up and pay on the gate and go in the home sections if necessary. I did go onto add that in the whole these would be ordinary fair minded fans not looking for trouble but just wanting to get in and watch their team play football.

Got him by the balls, the police jumped in and said that for safety reasons they would be insisting that the game would now have to be all ticket to prevent possible crowd disorder that may occur if the fans were allowed to purchase tickets on the day. They could understand that Cardiff fans without tickets and wanting to see the game would simply pay for admission into the home sections and that there would be a huge potential for crowd disorder.

The floundering Eddie then jumped in with his solution and said that they would turn away any Cardiff fans from the home turnstiles thus preventing any of them from entering, it did bring a smile to the police men's faces when I asked how would he recognise the Cardiff fans, and did he expect them all to turn up in one group sing Men of Harlech, waving Welsh flags and eating leeks, the man had dug himself a hole for himself by being so stubborn. You could see the reality of the situation he'd caused hitting home to him.

Not only was he turning away a possible extra fifteen hundred Cardiff fans at around twenty pounds a head, but by his own admission the home crowd would be reduced by another three or four thousand by making the game all ticket and preventing any match day walk up admission. So all in all a loss of somewhere around of over around one hundred thousand pounds, I wonder if his club Chairman ever got to hear of his stadium managers efforts to fill the tills, NOT.

In my opinion it is people like this who are destroying football as we know it, yes hooliganism if left un-checked would have destroyed the game, but hooliganism was more or less under control, the chaos of the seventies and eighties were long since passed. There are still situations that flare up on occasions up and down the country and yes they would still be classed by most as hooliganism, but days of having trains trashed week in week out, and mass street fights and town centres being turned over looted and damaged are long gone.

Of course there are lots of people who would like to return to such times, I was there I grew up through that period and it can be empowering and exciting to be part of a huge mob and seemingly invincible and unstoppable, this doesn't just apply to football, regularly you will see protests and demonstrations etc. escalate in to full blown riots.

The crowds involved will be made up like football crowds of some hardcore hooligans/anarchists call them what you want, there will also be a fair percentage of people who hadn't gone there looking for trouble, but now that it had started they would take advantage of the situation, these type of people may mindlessly damage anything they could whilst others would loot or steal anything they could get their hands on.

Another category would have no criminal intentions but just get caught up in the excitement/fear situation, either way the adrenaline involve in the fight or flight scenario would kick in and people would get swept along in events.

However in my experience and this is something we tried to encourage at the Valley Rams was a level of self policing and common sense. Each generation throws up a new breed of young hot heads who either don't know how to behave or often feel they have something to prove just to fit in with what they envisage is the "cool older scene".These are the kids that need to be kept in check and shown the ropes or the back of your hand if need be. The older wiser ones amongst us need to realise that we can't stand back and let others spoil things for us.For too many years to remember myself and many others around my age have been treated like lepers on our travels, service stations on route and pubs anywhere within a twenty mile radius of our intended visit would have the shutters up and be on full military alert.

One occasion that highlights the stupidity of some amongst us was at a game in Torquay late seventies early eighties. Now for some reason Torquay used to play their Saturday home games at 6pm, now this had risk all over it. Lots of us made a weekend of it and stayed over, lots travelled on the day, but set off the same time as they would have for a 3pm kick off, therefore an extra 3 hours drinking time at a sunny holiday resort, quite a heady mix.

Well the whole town was mental, I have never seen so many drunk Cardiff fans in one place. Just before kick off we called into a pub near the ground, well it was pandemonium, people were dancing on the pool table, swinging on the lights, the carpet had more glass on it than Trafalgar square after the poll tax riots, absolute mayhem.

Can't remember much about the game, other than a full scale pitch invasion to terrorise even more, the few home fans that had the audacity to turn up at their own stadium.

On the way out of the ground and making our way back to our accommodation (which was the back of our transit van parked up in the station car park for the weekend) we passed the same pub that had been wrecked earlier. Now trying to get into this well and truly locked up pub were the very same lads who 2 hours earlier had been swinging off the light fittings, I could hear the landlord telling them to piss off from behind the safety of his locked door and some of the lads replying, they promised to behave this time and they were only having fun and asking him if he'd lost his sense of humour. Fucking priceless, they were genuinely surprised that he wouldn't let them back in.

Unfortunately this story was repeated in many pubs that night and it amazed me that so many of our fans were surprised. During these days I could never envisage being allowed let alone welcomed into pubs and clubs on our travel, but we did help to change things and we need to protect the in roads we have made, we can't sit back and let the lunatics take over the asylum.

Whilst I'm writing and reading this myself as I go along, I feel like I'm making myself out to be some sort of "right wing do gooder" who's never crossed the line, but I don't see myself as one and I'm sure lots of people that know me, know differently. I love a laugh, I love that craic and banter, I have been pissed too often to recount and got caught up in more scrapes than I'd like to mention, but I have never understood the "shitting on your own doorstep mentality".

If we want to be allowed to travel and drink anywhere and everywhere we wish, then we have to accept there is a responsibility that goes with those privileges, we are still hit with harder and more sanctions than any other club in the country and we are consistently walking a tight rope and then when you get stupid prats throwing coins at a referee as they did with our home match with Swansea this year we go two steps forward and the take a giant step back.

We're still marching on, we might not be as one big Rams
supporters club but we will still always follow The City

Now the younger ones have gone their own way
since the Rams no longer exist

Chapter 9
The solution to the problem

There isn't one solution! But also so, there isn't just the one problem. I don't feel qualified enough to discuss the psychology behind the "football hooligan scene" there have been plenty of academics who have covered the why's and wherefore's of that, however I do feel justified in drawing some of my own conclusions gathered from my experiences and involvement at both ends of the scale.

What has become more apparent over recent years and not just at football is the Big Brother total conformity to the system attitude. You no longer have to commit a crime or break a law to attract heavy handed policing, you will be seen and treated as a threat just for not following the master plan laid out for whatever game or event is planned.

This situation has been imposed on our fans so many times, when you will have a match plan laid out by some highly educated senior officer sat behind his desk using all his knowledge gained by attending his one match during his training period and that was Chester versus Torquay United so he knows all about football hooliganism. He will draw up the master plan that states all fans will come on official coaches they will rendezvous at a set location where they will sit patiently and quietly until all the coaches have arrived, anyone asking to stretch their legs use the toilets or go to the shops will be treated as criminals and dealt with accordingly.

What frustrates me so much is the mindset of some police Officers but also the mindset of some fans. Not all football fans are mindless hooligans who are a threat to society. Equally so, not all police officers are right wing fascist thugs. But in defence of the fans, they aren't a trained highly paid professional body, the police on the other hand are.

Football fans to me represent the widest and best cross section of society. Part of the appeal to me at football is the bringing together of such a broad cross section of people. Football is an escape from the humdrum and pressures that every day life can throw up, at Cardiff amongst our regular travelling fans who you get to know, we have many professional people, Doctors, Solicitors even off duty Policemen, we have a broad mix of colours and creeds, but when we are together all I and others see is a group of fellow City fans. When we score a goal or win a tense game and people are hugging one another in a mass loved up mosh pit, people who are usually quite shy and private, suddenly they are hugging people they've only just met as if they are brothers, and in truth for that small moment in time they are brothers and the term football family is not a term I use lightly, but that sums up the position perfectly, the sense of belonging to this family should not be under estimated.

Now we can look at many factors behind our whole make up at Cardiff, the rough working class background, the tribal feeling of being Welsh and seen as different, the lay out of the hundreds of small valley towns that supply such a large percentage of the Cardiff support. Lots of facts make us a little more unique than many others sets of fans and possibly the factors make us a closer tighter knit family, also the years of crap football we have endured together must have played a part in the togetherness we share.

This togetherness is seen by some as a threat; it does spill over sometimes as I have covered earlier but very, very rarely nowadays. We as fans have to play our part in helping to keep the enthusiasm and power we create in check, but unfortunately often we aren't given the chance and we are pre judged and treated as a threat before anything has even happened.

This leads to a catch 22 vicious circle scenario. We get treated badly and heavy handedly and we respond with a similar attitude. I get so fed up of hearing high ranked officers using the term "we will treat the Cardiff fans with a firm but fair approach", and the reality of that is, you will be intimidated, pushed and shouted at and if you don't like it and respond then you will get whacked and arrested. So that's fair enough then.

Why not treat people well, give them the benefit of the doubt and some trust and then, if they abuse those privileges deal with it accordingly. But forgive me for repeating myself, push us and we push back, hit one of us unjustly and you will have to fight all of us. People who are nowhere near what you'd describe as hooligans, will not stand by and see fellow fans being treated unjustly in a heavy handed manner. These people are the ones we need to keep on board. But often what happens is the "normal" average fair minded person suddenly sees a rogue policeman lashing out or being unfair and the them and us picture gets drawn. The police are there to maintain order and protect society, but as we see too often and especially at football they are alienating themselves and becoming the enemy of the majority, rather than solving the problems caused by the minority.

One of the major frustrations especially on match days is the lack of communication and lack of getting any form of redress if there has been a case of mistreatment of our fans. I am sure we have all seen fans asking for an officers number or asking to speak to a higher ranking officer to make a complaint and you can just see the blank look you are treated with. As if you are shit on someone's shoes. We can have photographs, video recording or incidents witnessed by dozens of law abiding citizens, but it all falls on deaf ears and each occasion just helps to further the distance between the two groups. It really is an eye opener when people come along to a game not knowing what happens in the real world of a football fan. You will hear these newbie's saying "they can't do that" and "surely you can report them". It can be quite funny when you see one of them approach a copper and say something along the lines of "Excuse me Officer, I think you are being rather heavy handed with the methods you are adopting", only to be pushed in the chest, told to fuck off over there or you'll get locked up. Welcome to the world of the football fan.

What would help is a bit of consistency amongst the police forces from each area. Actually it can even differ within the area for some reason. I remember two games played away in a short period, one was at Sheffield United on the Saturday, where it was policed in a party mood and it was spot on. We had encountered loads of problems at Sheffield united over the previous two games, but for this game the police involved came to meet us to discuss some alternative methods to police us for this game. They allowed us to drink in Rotherham pre match. They mixed with us and chatted in friendly methods and it worked a treat. Four days later we were back in Sheffield but this time playing Sheffield Wednesday, same city, same police force but a different match commander and my God what a different approach. It was like a war zone, every bus on arrival was met by a police dog coming up the steps to meet you.

I was waiting on the forecourt of the stadium for the buses to arrive; I had some tickets for some lads on different buses and also had to pay the drivers as they arrived.Out of the blue a copper grabbed me by the collar and told me to "fuck off into the ground you Welsh C—t or you're nicked". Some of our club stewards were close by and saw these events. I told the copper involved to get his fucking hands off or I'd do it for him. A sergeant standing close by saw this and said "book him and do him with a fixed penalty". I told him he could shove the fixed penalty up his arse and if he wanted to arrest me then do it properly and let's have our day in court.

One of our stewards seeing this unfolding had got hold of our FIO's and they came over. Wayne the Sergeant said "what's the problem Gwyn?" Their sergeant said "oh you know him do you?" and Wayne told him of course he did as I had organised 70% of the coaches that were up that night. One of the stewards told Wayne what had happened and you could see the colour draining from the faces of the Sheffield coppers. They back tracked now and said they wouldn't pursue the matter, which was about the closest anyone would get to an apology. I was absolutely bouncing, but bit my tongue not to cause any more problems and put our coppers on the spot.

It really hit home to me the whole unfairness of such situations. I was lucky to be known by our stewards and police and had some level of protection, but other than that I would have been nicked and had the normal "firm but fair" treatment and been left with a three year ban.

When things were taking shape in the early Rams days, I started to think that I could make a difference. I thought we could help to get fair play and better treatment for our fans as long as they played their part. Sadly we were betrayed and simply lied to by so many forces, that for every step forward we would take, we would then go to an area such as the West Midlands and be dragged back two steps.

It wouldn't always wash with our lads. When I would say we can't take it out on the police in Norwich, just because the police in Wolves were a bunch of knobs. Sadly some fans judge all the police in the same category, just as some police see all football fans as hooligans. How we change those perceptions I don't know, but having one senior officer who can be responsible for the football policing nationally would help, but it will never happen and the internal politics and one upmanship that goes on from area to area has to be seen to be believed.

Some things that have been picked up on by some of our older more switched on fans are the more we comply, the pettier the police and the charges become. In other words when we would turn up mob handed and there was genuine threat of real trouble as there was in the 60's through to the 90's. During those days the police were to busy preventing real hooliganism and disorder from breaking out, they also new that if they steamed in to the middle of a mob to grab someone, usually the whole mob would become involved and often they would look at the broader picture and individuals would escape arrest accordingly.

It has now gone full circle and in most cases where people comply in general, you will see police men picking out targets for minor things such as littering, swearing and drinking on the street etc. often if the police simply don't like the look of you or feel you have a bit of an attitude, then they will pull you and arrest you for anything they wish such as drunk entry into a football stadium or one of the many disorder sections they wish to trump up.

They have even brought out laws now that allow them to simply send you back home if they feel you could possibly have a drink and could possibly cause problems, my god how do you get out of that one. They may as well take everyone's driving licences off us now because we may possibly break the speed limits in the near future.

What concerns me is people and not just at football will simply say enough is enough and without getting to political, anarchy will break out. You simply can't go around alienating lot's of people who in the main are decent law abiding people, what is happening as I see it is instead of alienating the scumbags and bad people of this world, they are driving more of us into a corner alongside these people who should be seen as the real enemy.

There is no place in football for people who throw objects on the pitch, trash pubs and premises up and down the country, bully people and cause genuine serious disorder. But whilst the police continue with their current approach the them and us attitude will continue and a lot of decent people will not know which side of them and us they belong to.

I may be repeating myself, but the Police are the well paid well trained professionals, they must set the right examples I hope we can get some common sense and middle ground approach, but I wont beholding my breath I'll just be keeping my head down, trying not to get caught up in the lottery that is involved in being a football fan.

Mel in the whoops before his arm was broken

Reservoir Dogs, Ant Hill mob style

Tex and Joey Mullins

Jinx and Davies. My two right hand men

The future is bright!

The following books are available:

"From Shattered Dreams to Wembley Way"
By Annis Abraham Jnr
£16.99p incl p&p

"The Diary of The Real Soul Crew"
By Annis Abraham Jnr
£9.99p incl p&p

"The Diary of The Soul Crew 2"
By Annis Abraham Jnr
£9.99p incl p&p

"Cardiff City Fans Through The Years"
By Annis Abraham Jnr
£11.99p incl p&p

at
www.annisabraham.co.uk